BEN PATTERSON

DEEPENING YOUR

CONVERSATION

WITH GOD

Learning to Love to Pray

D0030004

DATE DUE

"With seductive simplicity and vulnerability, Ben Patter-son's book made me yearn for the depths of joy prayer can bring. God's grace and infinite worth resonate from every page with the message that knowing him is both a journey and destination worth leaving everything for."

Tricia McCary Rhodes
Author, *Taking Up Your Cross*

"Reading this book was a refreshing scriptural experience. I have sent many copies to my friends. After you read this volume I'm sure you will, too."

H. Norman Wright
Founder and Director, Christian
Marriage Enrichment
Author, *The Complete Book of
Christian Wedding Vows*

"We have not because we ask not. This wonderful book on prayer, by a man who has learned its beauty from hard yet poignant experience, both teaches us how to ask and makes us desire to do so."

Dr. Daniel Taylor
Professor of English,
Bethel College

"God desires a closer relationship with us, his children. Ben Patterson provides some wonderful insights to help us draw nearer to him. Nothing is more important than knowing God and developing an intimate relationship with him."

Dr. Bill Bright
Founder and President,
Campus Crusade for Christ

DEEPENING YOUR CONVERSATION WITH GOD

Learning to Love to Pray

BEN PATTERSON

BETHANY HOUSE PUBLISHERS
MINNEAPOLIS, MINNESOTA 55438

Published by Bethany House Publishers
A Ministry of Bethany Fellowship International
11400 Hampshire Avenue South
Bloomington, Minnesota 55438
www.bethanyhouse.com

Printed in the United States of America by
Bethany Press International, Bloomington, Minnesota 55438

Library of Congress Cataloging-in-Publication Data

Patterson, Ben, 1942–
    Deepening your conversation with God : learning to love to pray / by
Ben Patterson.
        p.   cm.
Includes bibliographical references.
    ISBN 0-7642-2351-8
    1. Clergy—Religious life. 2. Prayer—Christianity. 3. Pastoral
theology. I. Title.
    BV4011.6 .P38 2001
248.8'92—dc21

                                                            2001001258

To the Hope College Campus Ministries Staff
Partners in Prayer,
Sailors on the ocean of God's glory,
Laughers!

Paul,
Dolores,
Dwight,
Tim,
Darnisha,
Lori,
Cheri,
Dani.

Soli Deo Gloria

BEN PATTERSON is campus pastor at Westmont College in Santa Barbara, California. He has served churches in New Jersey and California and was dean of the chapel at Hope College in Michigan before going to Westmont College. He is the author of *Waiting: Finding Hope When God Seems Silent* and is a back-page columnist for LEADERSHIP JOURNAL and a Contributor to *Christianity Today*.

PREFACE

THERE IS PERHAPS no greater evidence that human beings act contrary to their self-interest than the fact that we spend so little time talking to the one who made and loves us. An amazingly high percentage of Americans say they believe in God, but most can't find the time or the inclination to mutter much more than an occasional request for a small favor.

My early prayer life centered on the Los Angeles Dodgers. I lived most devoutly during baseball season and prayed most fervently during the late innings of ball games. My prayers consisted mostly of repetitive pleading and vague promises. In especially tough situations, I put my pillow over my head.

I am not sure that I have progressed very far from those early years. My best hope lies in my thirty-year friendship with Ben Patterson. God often illustrates for you in the life of another a blessing that he desires for you.

Over the years I have watched Ben move from a man whose life was marked by action followed at a distance by reflection to a man who understands that no action is as powerful as prayer. When he speaks of lying flat on his back on his living room floor while he prayed his way through his church roster, I remember both the floor and the debilitating injury that put him there. I remember the

7

amazing sense that I had never seen my football-playing, weight-lifting, bike-riding friend doing a more active thing in his high-energy life.

One of the most intriguing of the many fresh insights in this book is Ben's discussion of the shift in his perception of prayer as an important spiritual discipline to prayer as a much anticipated delight. I can admire a person who gets up in the early morning hours because prayer is important, but I hardly know what to make of a man who gets out of bed in the dark because the act of prayer is so pleasurable. Clearly, I have something to learn.

In order to learn to love to pray, as opposed to loving the idea of praying, one must experience the feeling while praying that you are at the center of reality. This runs contrary to common notions—that prayer, for instance, is a retreat from the real world, that prayer is a kind of luxury that we hope someday to be able to afford, that some people—the prayer warriors—have a gift for prayer that most of us lack.

Serious prayer is not a special gift, not even primarily a responsibility; it is a practical privilege—a privilege because it is an invitation to speak with the Creator of the universe, practical because nothing is more useful for giving our everyday lives weight and direction.

We have not because we ask not. This wonderful book on prayer, by a man who has learned its beauty from hard yet poignant experience, both teaches us how to ask and makes us desire to do so.

—Dr. Daniel W. Taylor
Professor of English
Bethel College
St. Paul, Minnesota

CONTENTS

INTRODUCTION

THERE WERE ABOUT five hundred college students in the auditorium on that muggy August night at Forest Home Christian Conference in Southern California. I have no idea what the other four hundred and ninety-nine were doing, but I know I was transfixed. An Oxford Ph.D., Dr. J. Edwin Orr, was delivering a lecture on the history of spiritual awakenings in North America and the role students, particularly praying students, had played in them.

Vivid in my memory was the story of the so-called 1806 Haystack Revival at Williams College in Massachusetts. It was so named because the little band of five students who wanted to pray that night were afraid to pray on campus. The hostility toward Christians was so intense that they even kept the minutes of their meetings hidden. So they went off campus to a nearby farm to pray for revival at their school. When a storm broke out, they burrowed under a haystack for protection. But their prayers were answered; revival came to Williams College not long afterward, and with it a powerful world missions movement. The youthful leader of that prayer group, Samuel Mills, would later become one of the founders of the American Board of Commissioners for Foreign Missions and the American Bible Society. Today there is a plaque on the site with the inscription: The Birthplace of Foreign Missions.

Only kids

What impressed me most was that these people were just kids, my age or younger. Already, at age nineteen, in the early '60s, I could identify with the statement of a somewhat disillusioned pastor: "Wherever Paul went there were riots. Wherever I go, they serve tea." Was it possible that God could use me that way, if I prayed?

Williams College was not unusual for that period, both in its corruption and in its revival. Regarding college dormitories, one historian likened them to "secret nurseries of vice and the cages of unclean birds." At one college, a hole was cut in the center of the president's Bible, so when he opened it, a deck of playing cards fell out. At another college, a drinking society named itself H.E.O.T.T., a parody of the words of Isaiah 55:1, "Ho, everyone that thirsteth."[1] And yet, as little bands of students prayed for God to do what mere humans could manifestly not do, things changed radically. Schools like Amherst, Dartmouth, Princeton, and Yale saw the conversion of a third to a half of their student bodies. And the changes were not limited to colleges. From top to bottom, American culture and morals were profoundly affected by these awakenings.

Still, as gripping as these stories were, it was an audacious thing for Orr to do what he did, lecturing for nearly two hours to five hundred students packed into a large room on a warm August evening. But Ben Patterson left the hall that night burning with a desire to see God do again what he did then. Since the tumultuous decade of the '60s was just beginning, I had no idea how relevant that yearning would become in the years ahead.

Nor could I anticipate how thoroughly that passion

---

[1]David McKenna, *The Coming Great Awakening* (Downer's Grove, Ill.: InterVarsity Press, 1990), 32–33.

would be leached out of me before that decade was over. I say this with tears of regret. I can sum up those years of my life with the title of Malcolm Muggeridge's autobiography, *Chronicles of Wasted Time*. The academic study of religion, the seminary experience, the emergence of psychology and sociology as alternative faiths, and my work in a mainline church—none of these were friendly to the vision of my naïve youth. They need not have been that way, but they were in my experience. Intellectual pride, religious professionalism, and the hubris of that most arrogant and narcissistic of decades in American history conspired to damage my soul.

I emerged from the '60s angry and confident. Like so many of that generation, I was captivated by the idea of institutional evil. I saw it everywhere: in politics, business, education, and religion—especially religion. Where my earlier piety saw the evil of institutions as the evil of the human heart writ large, my more secularized piety tended to see institutions as doing most of the writing. Fix the institutions, and you'll fix a lot of what's wrong with humans. My institutional field was the church. The church was pretty screwed up, I thought, thus the anger. I knew just what it needed: it needed me, thus the confidence. If only I could get my hands on the church for a while, I could fix it.

Life's two great tragedies

George Bernard Shaw wrote that there are two tragedies in life: one is not to get your heart's desire. The other is to get it. I've suffered both calamities. *If only I could get my hands on the church for a while, I could fix it.* And so in 1975, God gave me my heart's desire: he called me to start a new church in Irvine, California. I could start from the ground floor without the mistakes of predecessors to hamstring my creativity. I knew it wouldn't be easy. I was more than a little scared at the prospect, but I believed. This thing could be done! With some help from God, of course, and from a few friends with like vision, it could happen! We could build the church that would be the pinnacle to which two thousand years of Christian history had struggled to reach.

It took nearly seven years for me to lose confidence in myself. It came by way of two ruptured discs in the lumbar region of my back. The doctor had prescribed six weeks of total rest, just to determine whether surgery would be needed. My first thought was *OK, I guess I'll get a lot of reading done*. But due to the pain, the pain-killers, the muscle relaxants, and lying on my back, my eyes didn't focus well. I read one book in six weeks. And I couldn't lie in bed, either; it was too soft. So the six weeks were spent on the floor. The pain was horrible, and humiliating. A trip to the bathroom was a race between my bladder and my capacity for pain. Sometimes I had to lie down on the bathroom floor to recover from the trip before I could do what the trip was for.

I was of no use to the church, so I thought. I couldn't preach, I couldn't lead meetings, I couldn't make calls. I couldn't do anything but pray. So I asked my wife to bring me the new church directory with the pictures of all the church members in it. I decided I would pray for every member every day I was on the floor. It took nearly two hours for me to do this. Don't misunderstand: this wasn't great piety. Mainly I was bored and frustrated. But very quickly these times of prayer became sweet.

Toward the end of my convalescence, I had taken a walk and was back on the floor resting and thinking about going back to work. I said to the Lord, "You know, these times of prayer have been sweet. It's too bad I don't have time to do this when I'm at work." Then the Lord spoke. He addressed me: "Stupid." That was his word. He said it in a pleasant tone of voice, though. He said, "Stupid, you have the same twenty-four hours each day when you're sick as when you're well. The trouble with you, Ben, is when you're well, you think you're in charge; when you're sick, you know you're not."

God's room

He was right. That led me to consider how well I had been doing while I was in charge. The church I had hoped would be special, set apart, a city set on a hill for other churches to pattern themselves after, was turning out like all the others. By God's mercy it was and is a good church. The people are precious. But it's not special—or at least any more special than any number of other churches. Every mistake I swore I'd never make as a pastor I had made by then, and then some. Everything I swore would never happen in my church had happened by then, and then some. And most important: the world was still going to hell, and we appeared to be impotent to do anything about it, much less to stop it.

In many ways we were no different than the rest of the churches in North America. We had an abundance of resources. By any international standard, we were rich in education, land, money, media, technology, and programs. But was the city of Irvine appreciably different because we and the other churches in town were there? Not much, it seemed.

I had lost my confidence. But I was learning to pray again. My haystack was my living room floor. My Williams College was my city. Irvine Presbyterian Church was but a little flock, unequal to the task of building the kingdom of God. But it was to a little flock that Jesus said, "Fear not, little flock, for your Father has been pleased to give you the kingdom" (Luke 12:32). We don't build the kingdom, Christ does. It isn't an acquisition, it's a gift. And I was coming to the conviction that if I can build a church, it isn't worth building. I'm in my mid-fifties as I write this. I feel about my age as Lou Holtz said he felt about coaching at the University of Minnesota: It isn't the end of the world, but you can see it from here. Perhaps I have several good, productive years of ministry left in me. God only knows. But whatever the time I have left, I want only to do the things I can't do unless God does it. I want there to be an abundance of what Bob Pierce called "God room" in all my endeavors. For Pierce, "God room" was the gap between what we can do by ourselves and what can only happen if God steps in. Yes. That's it. That's what I want.

Worst sin

I shudder at my capacity for presumption. Did I really think I could do this thing called ministry on my own, or with only a little help from my Friend? P. T. Forsyth said, "Prayerlessness is the worst sin, because it bespeaks as nothing else does, that root of all sin: 'For although they knew God, they neither glorified him as God nor gave thanks to him'" (Rom. 1:21).[2]

I must confess my prayerlessness the way Kierkegaard confessed his sins:

> Father in heaven! Hold not our sins up against us but hold us up against our sins, so that the

---

[2]P. T. Forsyth, *The Soul of Prayer* (Grand Rapids: Eerdmans, 1916), 11.

thought of Thee when it wakens in our soul, and each time it wakens, should not remind us of what we have committed but of what Thou didst forgive, not of how we went astray but of how Thou didst save us![3]

Have mercy, Lord. Hold me up, indeed.

I was in great need of being held up the night I was ordained into the ministry. It was another balmy night, in May this time, in La Jolla, California. I was decked out in a black robe, sweating profusely as I knelt on the carpet of the church's sanctuary, and about twenty elders laid their hands on me to pray. I typically don't ever kneel to pray; it hurts my knees and my legs tend to cramp. Both were happening that evening. The combined weight of all those hands was pressing me into that carpet and bending me over. And the prayers! Long and sonorous. I needed air! I needed to stand up! I needed to run outside and tear off that infernal robe! It was altogether prophetic of what was to come in the ministry in the years ahead.

And so was what followed. I was on the verge of struggling to my feet and making the first official act of my ministry—the closing of the meeting—when my senior pastor began to pray, "Lord, as Ben feels the weight of these hands . . ." I was listening. He continued, "May he also feel the weight of responsibility that is his." I groaned, and prepared again to get up. Then he prayed, "But may he also feel the strength of your everlasting arms holding him up." I stayed on my knees and murmured an amen.

Staying on my knees. It was hard that night, it's been hard ever since. Mary Slessor was right about prayer: "Praying is harder work than doing . . . but the dynamic lies that

[3] Sören Kierkegaard, *The Prayers of Kierkegaard*, Perry D. LeFevre, ed. (Chicago: The University of Chicago Press, 1956), 21.

way to advance the kingdom."[4] The weight of all those hands, the heat and the pressure, my weakness and rebelliousness—all these make ministry an impossibility, unless there are everlasting arms to hold me up.

Not into prayer

I'm not "into" prayer. I seem to have missed the religious gene or whatever it is that makes people enjoy the act of praying. It's not my nature to pray. *I'm not into prayer, I am into God!* I thirst and hunger for God, I ache for God. Without his everlasting arms holding me up, I will fall. So I must pray. I must daily and moment by moment pray in one way or another the words the pilgrims to Jerusalem prayed:

> Unless the Lord builds a house,
>   the work of the builders is useless.
> Unless the Lord protects a city,
>   guarding it with sentries will do no good.
> It is useless for you to work so hard
>   from early morning until late at night,
> anxiously working for food to eat;
>   for God gives rest to his loved ones.
>   (Ps. 127:1–2 NLT)

---

[4]Quoted in Basil Miller, *Mary Slessor* (Minneapolis: Bethany House Publishers, 1974), 138.

WHY PRAY?

HE WAS A SEASONED VETERAN of the Christian ministry, my first boss, a respected mentor, a dear friend, and on the edge of retirement. I had asked him what were the most important lessons he had learned in his years of following Christ. His answer came quickly: "Don't take it personally."

"Don't take what personally?" was my next question.

He told me not to take it personally when things get tough in the Christian life, when I am attacked or tired or depressed. Things like that go with the territory. We're in a spiritual battle. When a soldier is shot at, he isn't shocked. His feelings aren't hurt. He doesn't peer over his foxhole at his adversary and shout, "Was it something I said?" He expects it, he plans on it.

That's spiritual realism. That's what impelled Paul to write the Ephesians that "our struggle is not against flesh and blood, but against the rulers, against the authorities, against the powers of this dark world and against the spiritual forces of evil in the heavenly realms" (Eph. 6:12). Note that the apostle assumes his readers already know that the work of the kingdom is a struggle. He doesn't need to argue the point. The question is not whether we're in a battle, but what kind. The battle is spiritual. So we don't take it personally, we don't get hurt feelings when things get hard. We are spiritual realists.

Hunting lions with a squirt gun

And realists that we are, we do something else. We pray. Paul urges us to remember this when he tells us to put on the full armor of God, to wear such things as truth for a belt, righteousness for a breastplate, the gospel of peace for shoes, faith for a shield, and salvation for a helmet. The sword is also of the Spirit—the Word of God. Prayer plays a pivotal and unique role in all of this. For how does one put on the armor or wield the sword? By praying "in the Spirit on all occasions with all kinds of prayers and requests" (Eph. 6:18).

The command to pray is one of the few truly central and radical things God has called us to do in this spiritual warfare. It is central because it stands at the hub, the heart of our struggle. It's not all we are to be about, for there are many other wonderful and critical things to do in this spiritual warfare, such as preach the gospel, cast out demons, feed the hungry, care for the poor. But these great things are to prayer what the spokes of a wheel are to the hub. When the hub weakens, the rest of the wheel collapses. "You can do more than pray, after you have prayed," wrote A. J. Gordon, "but you can never do more than pray until you have prayed."[1] It is a divinely ordered sequence. When Jesus called the Twelve, he called them so that they might do three things. The first was simply to "be with him."

---

[1] Source unknown.

With that in place, and from that place, he sent them out to do the rest: "to preach and to have authority to drive out demons" (Mark 3:14–15). All the work of the kingdom of God begins with simply being with Jesus. If it doesn't start there, it doesn't start at all.

The elders of the first church in Jerusalem understood this when they got so busy feeding widows and orphans that they weren't praying as they should (Acts 6:1–7). So they reorganized the church and delegated the feeding program to others, not because it was beneath them, but because it was so important. If prayer was crowded out of its central place in the church, so too would be the widows one day.

Bambi vs. Godzilla

To pray is also to engage in radical warfare. Merely human action touches only the surface of things, but prayer gets past the veneer, past mere appearances to the root of the matter. To make this point and to encourage us therefore to persist in prayer, Jesus told the story of a confrontation between a desperate widow and a heartless judge, opposites in a world in which relationships are calibrated according to power ratios (Luke 18:1–8). The widow is raw weakness. The judge is raw and callous power. She needs his help against a ruthless oppressor. He won't give it, for he neither fears God nor cares about people.

What happens in this world when raw weakness meets raw power?

In the '60s there was a popular cartoon short called "Bambi Meets Godzilla." It opened with a cute little baby deer grazing in a flowery meadow. Idyllic music played in the background. Then a shadow came across the screen. It was the monster Godzilla! The little deer looked up innocently at the beast. The monster glared back as its giant foot came down and crushed him. End of cartoon. That's the way it is in the world. When weakness meets raw, callous power, it's Bambi meets Godzilla. Children are abused, whole peoples are enslaved and marginalized, senseless wars are fought, hatred is passed from generation to generation. The evil is endless and inexorable.

But Jesus' story has a surprise ending. The widow persistently pleads her case and finally gets justice, despite the judge's callousness. A victory is won! That's what prayer does, says the Lord. It's radical, it goes down deep beneath the surface to uproot evil and upset the status quo. History and the future belong to the intercessors.[2] That's because the real struggle is spiritual, not physical. Those who know this are the true subversives, guerrillas of the Spirit, moving kingdoms and creation from their knees.

Whose work it is

So we pray—we must pray—because we are in a spiritual struggle—that we must take very, very seriously. We must pray for another reason: the work of the church is God's work, not ours. Jesus made that fact clear from the very inception of the church. He asked his disciples who people were saying he was. They gave the report: some were saying he was John the Baptist, others were saying he perhaps was Jeremiah or Elijah or another one of the prophets. Then he asked the biggest question God ever asks anyone: "But what about you? Who do you say I am?" Simon Peter shot his hand up to answer that one. He said, "You

---

[2]To borrow a phrase of Berkhof Hedrikus in his book *Christ and the Powers* (Herald Press, 1977).

are the Christ, the Son of the living God" (Matthew 16:13–16).

Pay close attention to what Jesus said in response to this first confession of faith in him. He first clarified how Peter came upon this momentous discovery. He let him know that it was not a conclusion that Peter arrived at on his own. He didn't figure it out because he had spent so much time with Jesus, listening to what he said, watching his miracles. "Blessed are you, Simon son of Jonah, *for this was not revealed to you by man, but by my Father in heaven*" (v. 17, italics mine). Merely to have spent a lot of time with Jesus, up close and personal, as great as that must have been, was not sufficient for Peter to apprehend who Jesus was. It required a supernatural event, a divine revelation. God's work begins with God, not humankind.

And so his work continues, for Jesus added, "And I tell you that you are Peter, and on this rock *I will build my church*" (v. 18, italics mine). Of course we must pray! If God is the builder and we are his servants in the building of his church, it is presumptuous to build without prayer.

And completely ineffective. Jesus came down the Mount of Transfiguration to an argument his disciples were having with the teachers of the law. They were unable to heal a demonized boy, a pathetic child who was periodically seized by an evil spirit and thrown to the ground, foaming at the mouth. When Jesus was told what the uproar was about, he said something he must often feel when he looks at his prayerless church: "O unbelieving generation . . . how long shall I stay with you? How long shall I put up with you? Bring the boy to me" (Mark 9:19). Then he healed the boy.

When the excitement died down enough for them to ask the question, his disciples said, "Why couldn't we drive it out?" Jesus' answer is as devastating as it is brief. He said,

"This kind can come out only by prayer" (Mark 9:29). They had to pray to drive the demon out! What on earth *were* they doing before Jesus walked up? Whatever it was, clearly they weren't praying. They were trying to cast out demons without prayer!

Reversed thunder

Churches can run without prayer. Whole denominations can run without prayer. The question is: Is what they're doing worth doing if they can do it without prayer? I don't think so. Jesus commissioned his church to storm the gates of hell. The world is still full of the "this kind" that Jesus confronted in the story of the demonized boy. Evil and darkness are as intractable and entrenched as they were in the first century. Do we really believe that programs and committees and ecclesiastical exertions and pronouncements are going to change that? Jesus doesn't. I think that when he's not bored with them, he's as angry as he was that day with his disciples. Nor should we believe in them. "This kind" will come out only by the power of God—that is, by prayer!

So we must pray, because the work of the church is God's work, not ours! We must also pray because prayer actually gets God's work done. That's the way prayer is seen in heaven. Ponder this scene in the throne room of heaven: An angel stands before God holding a golden censer, burning incense that is mixed with the prayers of the saints on earth. These prayers go up before God, and then are mixed with fire from the altar and hurled back down on earth. The amazing result is cataclysm on earth, "peals of thunder, rumblings, flashes of lightning and an earthquake" (Rev. 8:5).

Now picture the saints on earth, huddled in their

prayer meetings. If their experience of prayer is anything like mine can be, they may often feel their prayers are barely making it to the ceiling, or are dribbling out and rustling across the floor like dry leaves. Prayer doesn't frequently bring with it the sensation of cosmic power unleashed, what poet George Herbert called "reversed thunder." But that is exactly what is happening! The whole creation is shaken by the prayers of the saints. Something is happening as they pray. Work is being done, whether they see it or not.

Or consider the words of Paul to Timothy in his first letter:

> I urge, then, first of all, that requests, prayers, intercession and thanksgiving be made for everyone—for kings and all those in authority, that we may live peaceful and quiet lives in all godliness and holiness. (1 Tim. 2:1–2)

As first priority, Timothy's congregation is to pray for public officials that they make public policy decisions favorable to the church. Paul doesn't tell Timothy to pray that they be converted, although I'm sure he would be in favor of that kind of prayer too. He simply says to pray that these officials do the will of God, whether they know they are doing his will or not! This takes on even greater weight when we realize that the emperor at that time was the cruel madman Nero. Could a man like that actually do the will of God against his will? Paul tells Timothy to pray that he will. Clearly Paul believes prayer gets God's work done.

Harder work than doing

My favorite text in this regard is Paul's greeting at the end of his Colossian letter. He commends to his readers their pastor Epaphras, who is visiting Paul, and who is "always wrestling in prayer for you, that you may stand firm in all the will of God, mature and fully assured." Then he adds, "I vouch for him that he is working hard for you and for all those at Laodicea and Hierapolis" (Col. 4:12–13). What hard work could Epaphras possibly be doing for these people, while he is away from them? His wrestling in prayer for them is hard work. Prayer actually gets God's work done.

Mary Slessor was a missionary to West Africa in the nineteenth century. Her work among orphans there was nothing short of remarkable. Single and an activist, her days were long and arduous and at times lonely. She did the work of ten "normal" people in her lifetime. But she named prayer, not mere "doing," as the real dynamic of her accomplishments. In letters home to her friends she wrote:

> My life is one long, daily, hourly record of answered prayer. For physical health, for mental overstrain, for guidance given marvelously, for enmity to the gospel subdued, for food provided at the exact hour needed, for everything else that goes to make up life and my poor service. . . . I can testify with a full and often wonder-stricken awe that I . . . know God answers prayer. . . . Prayer is the greatest power God has put into our hands for service. Praying is harder work than doing . . . but the dynamic lies that way to advance the kingdom. I have no idea how and why God has carried me over so many hard places, and made these hordes submit to me . . . except in answer to prayer at home for me. It is all beyond my comprehension. The only way I can explain it is on the ground that I have been prayed for more than most. Pray on—power lies that way.[3]

---

[3]Basil Miller, 130, 138.

"Praying is harder work than doing." If Mary Slessor, the busy activist, could say that, it must be true. It is harder to pray than to simply "do." That's why Eugene Peterson says that the person who claims to be too busy to pray is really a lazy person. In busyness, he or she is procrastinating, avoiding the real work of prayer.

Why does God tell us to pray for the things he has promised to do anyway? For instance, he tells us to pray that his name will be hallowed and his kingdom come, things he has assured us he will bring to pass, anyway. After all, every knee shall bow and every tongue shall confess one day that Jesus Christ is Lord (Phil. 2:10–11). French philosopher and mathematician Blaise Pascal suggests that God does it to give us the dignity of causality. When my children were young, they would "help" me mow the lawn. The grass was too thick and the mower too heavy for them to push. So I stood over them, hands on the mower handle with theirs, my body bent slightly forward, and pushed as they "pushed" it through the grass. I could have done the job better and more easily alone, but I wanted the pleasure of their company. I also wanted them to have something to do that mattered, to have the dignity of causality. I think God commands us to pray for much the same reasons.

God's method

So we must pray, for prayer actually gets God's work done. We must also pray because prayer allows God to work on us. A great prayer text is 2 Corinthians 3:18: "And we, who with unveiled faces all reflect the Lord's glory, are being transformed into his likeness with ever-increasing glory."

To stand in the presence of God is, as it was with Moses'

shining face, to reflect his glory. Not only that, but it is to absorb his glory, to be transformed into his likeness. Like film in a camera, when the shutter opens to the light, we bear the likeness of the One who shines his light on us when we pray.

Perhaps one reason God delays his answers to our prayers is because he knows we need to be with him far more than we need the things we ask of him. I include myself among those who have prayed for years for someone or something with no apparent answer or resolution. But we can say that as we prayed long and hard, we found something we may not have been looking for when we began to pray, something better than the thing we asked of God. We found his incomparable presence. The praying can often be greater than the things we pray for.

Peter and John dazzled and scandalized the Sanhedrin with their courage when they were hauled before it to give an explanation for their wonder-working and preaching. After all, they hadn't been to seminary ("they were unschooled"). They weren't qualified to speak thus. Luke comments that the Sanhedrin "took note that *these men had been with Jesus*" (Acts 4:13, italics mine).

That's it! That's all we will ever really need to do the work of Jesus. The best thing we have to offer the world is not a college degree, not the communication classes we have taken, not the books we have read, not the success seminars and motivational workshops we have attended, but the fruit of our walk with the Lord—what is borne in us from the time we have spent with him. As helpful as these things can be, they are at best spokes in the wheel—but never the hub. That's why Dwight L. Moody said he would rather learn how to pray than how to preach. For Jesus' disciples never asked him to teach them how to preach, but how to pray. Beware the preacher, the theologian, the professor who does not pray.

From a wordly perspective, the church in North America is the best-equipped in history. It has more money, more books, more media tools than the church in any other place on earth. Yet with all this, the church overall is shrinking, not gaining in numbers. One has to go to the poor and uneducated countries of the earth, to places like East Africa and Latin America, to find a growing church. True, they need and desire leaders who are better educated. But in all this God seems to be saying to us something like the thing Jesus said to Martha, "You are worried and upset about many things, but *only one thing is needed*" (Luke 10:41–42, italics mine). The one absolutely essential, non-negotiable thing is to be with Jesus as Mary was. The church grows when its people attend to the one thing needed, not when it is preoccupied with the many things not needed.

That's because *people* are God's method, not techniques and programs. And people become usable to God only as they swell in his glorious presence. Emerson McKendree Bounds was alarmed at certain tendencies he saw in his denomination at the end of the nineteenth century. He would despair if he saw how what he then called a "trend of the day" has now become the order of the day:

> We are constantly on a stretch, if not on a strain, to devise new methods, new plans, new organizations to advance the church and secure enlargement and efficiency for the gospel. This trend of the day has a tendency to lose sight of the man or sink the man in the plan or organization. God's plan is to make much of the man, far more of him than of anything else. Men are God's method. The church is looking for better methods; God is looking for better men. . . . What the church needs today is not

more machinery or better, not new organizations or more and novel methods, but men whom the Holy Spirit can use—men of prayer, mighty in prayer. The Holy Spirit does not flow through methods, but through men. He does not come on machinery, but on men. He does not anoint plans, but men— men of prayer.[4]

So, we must pray! I recently went back to preach in the first church in which I worked, the place where I worked under my first boss, the man who told me not to take it personally, to remember the nature of the battle we are in. As I walked to the church on that Sunday morning, my mind was awash in memories, most of them embarrassing. Arrogant and foolish, I said and did many things there I wish I hadn't. But somehow God did some wonderful things both in and through me back then. Tears of gratitude and joy welled up in me. I said out loud to the Lord, "I was in over my head, wasn't I? You have been so faithful." I felt his smile with his rebuke as he answered, *"So what makes you think you're in your depth now?"*

I'm still in over my head. So are you. So we must pray.

---

[4]E. M. Bounds, *Power Through Prayer*, in *The Complete Works of E. M. Bounds on Prayer* (Grand Rapids: Baker Book House, 1990), 447.

2

OUR REAL WORK

GREAT BASEBALL CATCHER Yogi Berra played a game in which the score was tied with two outs in the bottom of the ninth inning. The batter from the opposing team stepped into the batting box and made the sign of the cross on home plate with his bat. Berra was a Catholic, too, but he wiped out the plate with his glove and said to the pious batter, "Why don't we let God just watch this game?"

Letting God just watch. That's good theology when applied to the outcome of a baseball game. It's terrible theology when applied to the way we live our lives and carry out the work of the church. Worse than that, it's fatal.

But too often that is precisely the outlook we bring to our vocation as Christians. God attends the game, but only as an honored spectator. Our prayers are merely ceremonial functions, like asking the President of the United States to throw out the first baseball at the beginning of baseball season, they are tips of the hat, verbal recognition over the loudspeaker between innings. He may even be in the dugout, but he rarely, if ever, gets on the playing field.

Are my words too strong? Not if I am to believe half of

what I hear from my colleagues about the weight and frequency assigned to the role of prayer in their work. Prayer is always getting nudged aside, neglected, or perfunctorily performed as more pressing concerns take center stage. Many of us feel we just have too much to do to have time to pray. That's the problem. We don't believe we are really doing anything when we pray—other than saying the words, that is.

That attitude is one of the most subtle and pernicious forms of worldliness infecting the church today. Why don't we believe we're getting anything done when we pray? Two reasons: the world's view and the world's pace.

All there is?

The world's view is basically a philosophical issue. It's the view of secularism; the notion that the material world is all there is; that reality is limited to what we can taste, touch, hear, smell, and see; and that we therefore live within a closed system of cause and effect, with nothing outside to influence what goes on inside. Such a worldview is suffocatingly claustrophobic. It is what sociologist Peter Berger called a "world without windows." G. K. Chesterton said it feels spiritually like what middle-aged businessmen feel after a big lunch. There can be no prayer in that kind of world, only spiritual slumber.

Of course, no Christian can be a secularist. But we can, however, be secularized. Secularism is a formal philosophical system. Secularization is a sociological reality. According to Os Guinness, it is a process by which religious ideas, institutions, and interpretations are losing practical social significance.

That last phrase is the operative one. For instance, it is fine to pray in your support group; it builds intimacy and warmth. But when we need to get something done in the church? That calls for practical things: committees, not prayer calls; talking, writing, telephoning, spending, budgeting, mobilizing, organizing, and mailing. And those kinds of things take time. So prayer gets preempted. It's a pleasant luxury that would be wonderful to spend more time on, if only we had the time to spend. But necessity presses in. After all, we have the budget to complete, the policies to formulate, and the proposals from the fellowship committee to act upon.

Not all there is

God's view couldn't be more opposed to that fatuous perspective. Our battle is not with these so-called necessities, but "against the rulers, against the authorities, against the powers of this dark world and against the spiritual forces of evil in the heavenly realms" (Eph. 6:12). We therefore fight a spiritual battle wearing spiritual armor and wielding spiritual weapons: the shield of faith, the breastplate of righteousness, the helmet of salvation, the belt of truth, the shoes of the gospel of peace, and the sword of the Spirit, which is the Word of God. (See Ephesians 6:13–17.)

Prayer plays a critical role in all of these. For how do we put on this armor? And how do we wield this sword? By praying "in the Spirit on all occasions with all kinds of prayers and requests" (Eph. 6:18). We put on the armor with prayer. We wield the Spirit's sword with prayer.

What if every church business meeting began with a reading of that passage from Paul? What if we really believed we were in the midst of a raging spiritual battle in which the stakes, the territory being fought over, is none other than ourselves and our people? What confidence would we place then in our organizational charts, lines of accountability and authority, budget reports, and plans for the Labor Day picnic? My hunch is that we'd all be too frightened not to pray. We'd all become foxhole Christians. Can there be any other kind?

It isn't that those business items are trivial; they are to be included in the responsibilities of Christian leaders. They are, however, trivial in comparison to our vocation to be men and women of prayer. To paraphrase Calvin Coolidge's famous remark about the business of America being business, the business of the church is to pray.

The hard and the soft

God's view is that there is one reality, but two dimensions: one seen, the other unseen (Col. 1:16.). But of the two, it is the unseen that is the larger and the more determinative. In fact, the seen is usually the arena in which the drama of unseen realities is being played out. It is the unseen that gives meaning to the seen. Rather than negating the seen, the unseen frames it and gives it a reference point. So Paul writes of his often difficult and discouraging work as an apostle in the realm of the seen, as being defined by the unseen:

> Therefore we do not lose heart. Though outwardly we are wasting away, yet inwardly we are being renewed day by day. For our light and momentary troubles are achieving for us an eternal glory that far outweighs them all. So we fix our eyes not on what is seen, but on what is unseen. For what is seen is temporary, but what is unseen is eternal. (2 Cor. 4:16–18)

When I was in college, we used to speak of so-called

hard courses and soft courses. The hard courses were the sciences, things like physics and biology, chemistry and math. The soft courses were things like philosophy and English, history and art. Hard meant fixed, solid, unchanging. Soft meant shifting, unsubstantial, ephemeral. But if change in the sciences has demonstrated anything in the last thirty years, it has shown just how changing these hard things are and how timeless the soft things are. Indeed, without the soft things, the hard things lose their meaning. So it is with the seen and the unseen.

When we lose God's view of things we lose perspective on everything else, too. Distinctions between the good, the better, and the best—even good and evil—grow fuzzy. A kind of radical egalitarianism takes over our responsibilities and activities, with anything and everything screaming for equal attention, equal time. Henry Zylstra was writing about life in the '60s, but what he said is truer now than it was then. If the proverbial anthropologist from Mars were to return from Earth to report to his planet on the religious culture of North America:

> [He] could do worse than take a copy of *Time* magazine with him, point to its table of contents, and say that what he had seen down here was a lot of people interested in: Art, Books, Cinema, Education, Medicine, Music, People, Personality, Press, Radio, Religion, Sports, Theatre . . . and the rest. If he were then asked whether the item called Religion, tucked in there between Radio and Sports, were the governing thing here . . . he would have to say that he thought it was not. He would have to say that Religion was operating alongside of those other things rather than in them and through them. . . . Presumably the man from Mars would have to report that religion, so far as serving as the

leaven which keeps the body of the national life from crumbling is itself one of the fragments.[1]

In this regard, the church has become a reflection of the culture, a thermometer instead of a thermostat. When prayer is moved to the periphery of the church, it can only mean that God has, too, and life becomes fragmented and very, very busy. For the world's view leads inevitably to the world's pace. The logic of secularization is busyness.

There is a sign on the Alaskan Highway that reads, "Choose your rut carefully. You'll be in it for the next 200 miles." The view that sees the material as all there is, or all that is of any practical value, creates a pace that is frantic at times, monotonous at others.

I read an article that, at the time, created a great deal of anxiety in me: "If You Are 35, You Have 500 Days to Live." Subtract the time you will spend sleeping, working, and tending to personal matters such as hygiene, odd chores, eating, and traveling. In the next 36 years you have 500 days of leisure. If this world is all there is, then none of us should waste our time praying. We should literally be grabbing for all the gusto we can get.

We see precisely that all around us. Yet, as leisure time increases, so do the problems of emptiness, boredom, and restlessness. We have, as a culture, a frantic determination to relax, unwind, and have fun. Where an earlier generation may have been compulsive about work, we are compulsive about what we do with our leisure time. We have made an idol of activity. Goethe's Faust is in many ways the quintessential modern. When he was trying to re-translate John 1:1, he searched for a more suitable equivalent to the Greek *logos* than "word." He settled on act. Thus: "In the

---

[1]Henry Zylstra, *A Testament of Vision* (Grand Rapids: Eerdmans, 1961), 181–82.

beginning was the Act, and the Act was with God, and the Act was God."

God's pace

God's pace is different. He says to us, " 'In repentance and rest is your salvation, in quietness and trust is your strength.' " But even as he says this, he knows how slow we are to believe it. He adds, " 'But you would have none of it.' " It's true, too true.

God parodies our solutions to our busyness: " 'You said, "No, we will flee on horses." Therefore you will flee! You said, "We will ride off on swift horses." Therefore your pursuers will be swift' " (Isa. 30:15–16). How do we try to solve our busyness? Why, we get busier! God's judgment is to hand us over to the logic of our choices. The faster we run, the faster our anxieties will run. Until, perhaps, we fall exhausted and let God be God.

Theologian Hans Küng wrote *On Being a Christian*, a 602-page theology of the Christian life, without a word about prayer. He was asked why, and he answered, in effect, "I forgot." There was the publisher's deadline, and the harassment he was receiving from the Vatican, and he over-looked prayer. Precisely. Prayer is always the first thing to go when we get caught up in the world's pace. And only prayer can deliver us from that pace.

Contrast that with Jesus. One day he is approached by a distraught father, a leader in the local synagogue, Jairus by name. His twelve-year-old daughter is dying. Would Jesus please come and help his little girl? If ever there was a 9–1–1 emergency, that was one.

So Jesus walks to his house. I had a friend remind me one busy day that Jesus walked just about everywhere he went. When he brought this to my attention, I said, "Of course he walked. He lived in the first century." But my friend smiled triumphantly and said, "Couldn't he have been born now, when he wouldn't have to walk everywhere? Wouldn't that have made so much more sense for the fulfilling of his mission on earth—to be born when he could have had a cellular telephone, a fax machine, and a word processor, access to air travel and the media? But doesn't the Bible say that he was born in the fullness of time, at the best possible moment in history? (Gal. 4:4). Clearly, he thought it was sufficient to come at a time when all he could do to get the message out was to walk places." Jesus didn't appear to be in nearly as big a hurry as I was.

On his way to Jairus's home, the crowd following him through the village street presses up against Jesus. Among them is a woman who has been suffering from a hemorrhage for years. She has it in her mind that if she can just touch Jesus' clothes, she'll get well. So she leans through the mass of bodies surrounding him and touches the hem of his robe. And the bleeding stops.

Jesus also stops. He looks around and says, "Who touched me?" His thoroughly secularized disciples say, "Master, the people are crowding and pressing against you." But Jesus insists: "Someone touched me; I know that power has gone out from me" (Luke 8:43–46). And the woman crawls trembling to his feet and explains everything. One gets the impression reading this story that Jesus actually chats with her awhile.

Have you ever wondered what Jairus was doing while Jesus was taking care of this woman? I have. Was he out of his mind with grief and impatience, gesturing silently for Jesus to get a move on? I think so. The woman can wait, his daughter can't. And, in fact, his girl does die.

But then Jesus walks to her and heals her, too.

Now, it would be a complete misreading of this story

to conclude: "Sure, Jesus can take his time. It's easy for him. He can raise the dead. He can miraculously do what didn't get done. But I can't." But the point of the story is not that Jesus can fix whatever got broken while he was distracted. The point is he never got distracted—and therefore he could take his time, because Jesus, the man of prayer, was perfectly in touch with his Father's will. He marched to the proverbial beat of a different drummer. He saw the seen through the perfect lens of the unseen.

And when he came to the end of his life, he could say to his Father with perfect calm and conviction, "I have brought you glory on earth by completing the work you gave me to do" (John 17:4). He got it all done! When was the last time you went to bed and looked back over a single day, feeling you could say you did all you were supposed to do? But there is always enough time to do what God wants us to do. The problem is we don't know what he wants because we're too busy doing what we think he *might* want done. It really wouldn't be a bad idea to ask him what he wants, would it? And then to listen?

Ora Labora

We would do well to take our clues from St. Benedict of Nursia. I first became aware of the Benedictines while driving across North Dakota one summer. Bored with the monotony of the Northern Plains, when my wife and I saw a church spire on the horizon, we turned off the interstate to see to whom it belonged. It was a Benedictine monastery. One of the brothers graciously gave us a tour. As we walked through the grounds and the buildings, I kept seeing the words *Ora Labora*. For all I knew, it was a kind of mouthwash. I was embarrassed at my ignorance, having gone to seminary and taken church history.

It took me a while to get up the courage to ask. What I heard has changed my life.

Benedict founded his Benedictine order as a reaction to the worldliness of the sixth-century church. His slogan was *Ora Labora*, from the Latin *ora*, "pray," and *labora*, "work." He taught his followers that to pray was to work, and to work was to pray. Following that rule, the Benedictine order broke down the artificial dichotomy between work and prayer. From there they also bridged the gap between the manual arts and the liberal arts, the physical and the intellectual, and the empirical and the speculative. A great tradition developed in which learning, science, agriculture, architecture, and art flourished. Much of what is considered beautiful "nature" in Europe today, particularly in France, was created by the Benedictine monks who drained swamps and cleared forests.

We must learn that prayer is our chief work. Only then can our work become prayer: real service, real satisfaction. This simple truth alone explains why so many people in the church find themselves exhausted, stretched to the breaking point, and burned out.

How often has our telling someone we'll pray for them been a cop-out? Meaning we won't do anything that really matters, anything concrete; or meaning we want to maintain a safe distance from them and their need.

Our prayer is our work! Only when that is true for us will our work be prayer: real worship, praise, adoration, and sacrifice. The classical postures of prayer, arms stretched out and hands open, or head bowed and hands folded, are gestures of openness and submission to God. They express perhaps the greatest paradox of prayer: that only when we give up on our human efforts can God's work begin and, mysteriously, human effort can come to fulfillment. As Ole Hallesby puts it in his book *Prayer*,

"Wherever we touch his Almighty arm, some of his omnip-otence streams in upon us, into our souls and into our bodies. And not only that, but, through us, it streams out to others."[2]

Ora Labora.

---

[2]Ole Hallesby, *Prayer* (Minneapolis: Augsburg Publishing House, 1963), 63.

3

TOO TIRED TO PRAY

ONE OF THE MOST REMARKABLE plants in nature is the *Ibervillea sonorae*. It can exist for seemingly indefinite periods without soil or even water. As Annie Dillard tells the story, one was kept in a display case at the New York Botanical Garden for seven years without soil or water. For seven springs it sent out little anticipatory shoots looking for water. Finding none, it simply dried up again, hoping for better luck next year.

Now that's what I call perseverance: hanging on, keeping on when it's not easy.

But perseverance has its limits, even for the *Ibervillea sonorae*. In its eighth year of no water, the rather sadistic scientists at the New York Botanical Gardens had a dead plant on their hands.

Most of us know what it's like to find ourselves past our seventh season, bereft of water, thirsty, and waiting for the eighth spring. No more energy and barely enough hope to send out one more pathetic little shoot. And it happens to us more like seven or eight times a year. Would that we could last like that tough little desert plant.

Sometimes it's simple fatigue that finally takes its toll. Too much work, a lingering illness, or poor diet come singly or in combination, and we find ourselves desperately in need of a good night's sleep, a day off, a walk in the park, or an antibiotic. That's all there is to it. Simple fatigue, simple treatment, and we snap back like a rubber band.

Deeper meaning

But there may be a deeper meaning to our thirst and fatigue. John Sanford paints a picture of this in his description of an old well that stood outside the front door of a family farmhouse in New Hampshire. The water from the well was remarkably pure and cold. No matter how hot the summer or how severe the drought, the well was always a source of refreshment and joy. The faithful old well was a big part of his memories of summer vacations at the farmhouse.

The years passed and eventually the farmhouse was modernized. Wiring brought electric lights, and indoor plumbing brought hot and cold running water. The old well was no longer needed, so it was sealed for use in possible future emergencies.

But one day, years later, Sanford had a hankering for the cold, pure water of his youth. So he unsealed the well and lowered a bucket for a nostalgic taste of the delightful refreshment he remembered. He was shocked to discover that the well that once had survived the severest droughts was bone dry! Perplexed, he began to ask questions of the locals who knew about these kinds of things. He learned that wells of that sort were fed by hundreds of tiny underground rivulets which seep a steady flow of water. As long as the water is drawn out of the well, new water will flow in through the rivulets, keeping them open for more to flow. But when the water stops flowing, the rivulets clog with mud and close up. The well dried up not because it was used too much, but because it wasn't used enough!

Sanford observed that our souls are like that well.[1] If we do not draw on the living water that Jesus promised would well up in us like a spring (John 7:38), our hearts close and dry up, and we find ourselves in our "eighth season." The consequence for not drinking deeply of God is to eventually lose the ability to drink at all. Prayerlessness is its own punishment, both its disease and its cause. That's the deeper meaning to our fatigue in the ministry.

Acedia

So like people dying of thirst in the desert, we stagger exhausted and aimless through our days. We have a vague sense of the things we ought to do, but we have forgotten why. This weariness comes close to what medieval theologians called the deadly sin of sloth or acedia. Simple fatigue says, "I know I should be doing this, but I just can't seem to generate the energy." Acedia says, "Why? What difference does it make?"

"Acedia is all of Friday consumed in getting out the Sunday bulletin," says Richard John Neuhaus in *Freedom for Ministry*. "Acedia is three hours dawdled away on *Time* magazine, which is then guiltily chalked up to 'study.' Acedia is evenings without number obliterated by television, evenings neither of entertainment nor of education, but of narcotized defense against time and duty. Above all, acedia is apathy, the refusal to engage the pathos of other lives

---

[1]John A. Sanford, *The Kingdom Within* (Philadelphia and New York: J. P. Lippincott Company, 1970), 15–16.

and of God's life with them."[2]

A physician friend gave me an article from the *Journal of Internal Medicine* that dealt with the psychological state conducive to illness called the "giving up, given up complex." It is found in people who lose the reasons for living; who are saying of their existence, "Why? What difference does it make?"

Acedia can make bodies vulnerable to disease and Christians terminally tired of religion, church, and even God.

Hyperactivity

Curiously, spiritual fatigue can produce what appears to be the opposite of sloth or acedia: hyperactivity. But in reality, it is just another dimension of the same thirst and sense of "why" that saps us of our ability to do the "what" of ministry. "Hyperactivity and sloth are twin sins,"[3] says Neuhaus, and rightly so. The only real difference is the anxious, frenetic shape hyperactivity takes. Too tired to pray, or too busy to pray: both are flip sides of the same coin. Either we stagger through our days exhausted and aimless like people dying of thirst in the desert; or like children lost in the woods, the more lost we feel, the faster we run.

Driving is the word that describes the schedules of so many of us who are no longer motivated to do the real work of the ministry. Hyperactivity is to authentic motivation as junk food is to a nourishing diet. It gives us the feeling of satisfaction while starving us to death. In the New Testament it is the Ephesian syndrome described in

---

[2]Richard John Neuhaus, *Freedom for Ministry*, revised edition (Grand Rapids: Eerdmans, 1992), 227.
[3]Neuhaus, Ibid., 228.

Revelation 2:1–7. The first love is gone, and now all that is left is the form and the trappings. This may be the malady most preyed upon by the innumerable seminars offered today on the techniques of church leadership. When we forget "why" we become obsessed with "how." Where once there was creativity and the tenderness born of deep love, there is now only the sex manual.

I crashed emotionally when I was twenty-six years old. I had dried up inside, and I was lost and running. Let's see if I can remember all I was doing: I was a full-time seminary student, head resident in the men's dorm at a local Christian college—that was full time, too—and I was working part time as the area director for Young Life in a nearby city. I was also on retainer as a speaker for a Christian conference center. In addition, my personal life was a contradiction to much of what I was preaching.

I came back to my room at the dorm one evening so tired I went straight to bed at eleven o'clock. That's early for a student living in a resident hall. Immediately I fell asleep and had a terrible nightmare. In the dream, I was backed into a corner by pale, ghoulish creatures who were plucking and tearing at my flesh, taking large chunks with each lunge. I awoke with a jerk and laid there for a while doing what I always do when I have a nightmare: I tried to talk myself back to reality. But I couldn't, because the dream was reality. I finally had to get up, get dressed, and walk around the dorm for a while just to get over the terror I felt. Only then could I go back to bed and go to sleep.

When I awoke the next morning, I felt like I had a hangover. (At that time in my life, I knew what a hangover felt like.) But I hadn't drunk anything the night before. To clear my head, I decided to walk over to the college track and go for a run. But when I got there, the gate was locked. I had climbed over the eight-foot fence many times, but this time it was just too much for me. If you would have seen me there that day you would have seen a young man bawling like a baby. The thought of one more thing to do was overwhelming.

When I stopped crying, I managed to climb over the fence and run for a while. My head a bit clearer, on my walk back to my room, I admitted to myself that I was in big trouble. The well was dry. I hadn't taken a drink of God in only he knew how long. I quit almost everything I was doing, got some help, made some fundamental changes in my outlook, and got on the road to health. One could say that for the next season of my life I took a pick and shovel and dug down deep to where the water had once flowed. It took a lot of sweat and work and coming to terms with no small amount of regrets, deep pain, and frustration. That's the way it usually is with repentance. But I thank God that I came to the point sooner rather than later; at twenty-six, instead of forty-six. For us in ministry, the stakes can only get higher as we get older and acquire more responsibilities.

Has the well gotten dry since? Never as bad as then. But it still does sometimes, and the way it usually shows itself is with hyperactivity. I know it's happening again when I go off to a quiet place for a day of prayer—and sleep all day, instead of pray. I'm so tired. It's a sign that it's been too long since I truly drank living water. With prayer, it can be like the so-called quality time I used to promise my spouse or children. It's a way I excuse myself from doing what I most need, but often least want, to do. As with my loved ones, so with prayer: there is no quality without quantity. No day of prayer can atone for weeks without prayer.

Hubris

The twin sins of acedia and hyperactivity can be expanded into triplets with the addition of a third: hubris. The Greeks used the word *hubris,* or pride, to speak of presumption, the folly of trying to be like the gods. This vice, rather than stemming from spiritual thirst and fatigue, is their essence. For the Christian, hubris is anything we do to try to save ourselves, including our attempts to fix our marriages, jobs, and the loves of others.

Hubris is bad enough by itself, but it also sets us up for acedia and hyperactivity. The greatest crisis I faced in my first church as a senior pastor came early, and it concerned the thing I most loved to do—preach. A pattern had developed in my weekly routine. Sunday afternoon through Monday morning I would be mildly to greatly depressed. Monday afternoon through Wednesday evening I would feel fine. Thursday I would begin to be a little irritable. The irritability would build on Friday, and on Saturday I would be very hard to live with. Then, voilà! On Sunday morning I would be transformed into the caring, engaging, and totally charming person everyone but my wife knew as Pastor Ben. Then, on Sunday afternoon, I would drop back into exhaustion and depression.

Week after week this cycle repeated itself. After a few months, I found myself vacillating between frenetic activity and paralyzing sloth—sometimes within the same day. I was bipolar spiritually and emotionally. I never doubted that God had called me to preach, but I was beginning to hate what I loved. Was this the way it was going to be the rest of my life? Living to do what I couldn't live with? Something had to change.

The insight came to me one day as I sat at my desk in my study. In the bookshelves directly across from me were the collected sermons of the preachers I revered: Spurgeon, Maclaren, Thielicke, bound in leather for posterity to read and to admire. Each week as I prepared to preach, it was as though they sat there in critical silence, measuring me and my words like a Ph.D. dissertation committee. I wanted so to please them—and to join them! I was trying each week to preach the world's greatest sermon; I wanted my sermons to be bound one day in leather for posterity to read and admire, too. That, I submit, is a terrible reason to preach. Instead of playing before an audience of one, God, I was playing before many: my people, my mentors, possible publishers, and generations to come. Superstardom escaped me each week, and the depression I felt each Sunday afternoon grew out of the disparity between what I sought and what I actually got. My sermonizing was clerical works-righteousness. Hubris had led me to shoot for fame instead of faithfulness. And it had me worn out and dry inside.

Prayer would be of inestimable value if it did nothing more than remind us of who we are before God. Unless the Lord builds the house, our work is useless (Psalm 127:1). Apart from him we can do nothing (John 15:5). Prayer is a reality check. It is impossible to both pray and be filled with hubris.

Remember why

Acedia, hyperactivity, hubris—all are forms of forgetfulness, of losing touch with the "why" and the "who" of ministry, of being cut off from the Vine, whose branches we are, and then keeping busy enough or noisy enough or narcotized enough not to have to face up to the fundamental disjointedness of our lives.

There is only one antidote to forgetfulness, and that is

remembrance. In Bunyan's *Pilgrim's Progress*, the pilgrims were leaving the Delectable Mountains after the shepherds warned them to beware of traversing the Enchanted Ground. The overwhelming desire there would be to fall asleep, never again to awake. And it was just as the shepherds told them it would be: the drowsiness there became nearly unbearable. Hopeful pleaded for a nap, just one little rest. But Christian made him talk. He asked him the question, "By what means were you led to go on this pilgrimage?" In other words, he asked, "Why are you on this journey? Why are you doing this?" By telling the story, and thus remembering why he was on the pilgrimage, Hopeful kept talking and kept walking.

It is remembrance that keeps us awake; it is significant that the supreme act of Christian worship, the Lord's Supper, draws us into fellowship with Christ by calling us to remember his mercy and love for us. It is a love feast spread out upon a redeemed and quickened memory. To pray is also to remember. It is to look into the face of the One who came to our side and saved us when we were lost and then called us into his service. It is to nourish the tender first love that Christ so passionately wants us to remember (Rev. 2:5). To pray is to connect again with the love that compelled us to declare the Good News to the world. To pray is to remember why we are doing this thing called ministry.

The trouble is, the more we need to remember why, the less we feel like remembering why. The more we need to pray, the less we want to. Not to pray is to lose the desire to pray, for prayerlessness is its own punishment. But pray we must. We cannot sit and wait for the desire to pray to suddenly come upon us like the tongues of fire at Pentecost. *Just do it*. The choices we make when we are not motivated are the most critical of our Christian walk. C. S.

Lewis touched on this when he had the devil Screwtape advise his nephew Wormwood that God sometimes overwhelms us with a sense of his presence early in our Christian experience, but that he never allows that to happen for too long. His goal is to get us to stand on our own two legs, "to carry out from the will alone duties which have lost all relish." Screwtape observes that during such "tough periods, much more than during the peak periods," we are growing into the creature God wants us to be.[4]

I cannot stress this too strongly: *Just do it.* You remember by remembering. You learn to pray like you learned to swim—not by talking about it but by getting in the water and splashing around. You relearn prayer the same way. Prayer is a discipline before it is a joy, and remains a discipline even after it becomes a joy. A friend, a champion wrestler, keeps a poster on the wall of his basement where he works out with weights. It shows a man straining to lift a weight, sweat fairly bursting from a grimacing face, veins bulging on his neck. The caption reads: "There are two kinds of pain: the pain of discipline, and the pain of regret."

How like life—and the life of prayer. To be alive is to hurt. The choice is not whether to hurt, but how. That you can choose. You can choose the discomfort of the discipline of praying when you don't feel like it, or the desolation and terminal fatigue of life without prayer.

Remember who

There's only one thing better than remembering why you're serving Christ; it's remembering who he is. It is he

---

[4]C. S. Lewis, *The Screwtape Letters* (New York: The Macmillan Company, 1944), 46–47.

who says to the weary and worn out, to the too-pooped-to-pray, "Come to me . . . and I will give you rest . . . and you will find rest for your souls" (Matt. 11:28–29). He knows how hard it is to do the work of the kingdom. He understands our exhaustion. He sympathizes with us even in our prayerlessness. Just to be with him is enough. There is no other one, no other place to go. "Lord, to whom shall we go? You have the words of eternal life" (John 6:68).

Luke has a marvelous line in his account of Peter and John's appearance before the Sanhedrin. He says the rulers, elders, and teachers of the law who sat in that august chamber were astonished at the courage of these un-schooled and ordinary men. The greatest thing we have to offer our people is not our education. It is not our good ideas. It isn't even our gifts and abilities. It is the fruit of the time we have spent with the Savior, the utterly unique and unparalleled thing that happens to us when we are simply in his presence.

Here is where prayer and work come together: The Christian life is a calling, a vocation. In fact, our English word vocation comes from the Latin *vocare*, which means "to call." The New Testament word with the same meaning is the Greek noun *klesis*. Thus the Greek for the church is *ekklesia*, from *ek*, "out of," and *klesis*, "a calling." God's people, the church, is the fellowship of the called. In the strictest sense of the word, the church is a vocational in-stitution. A crucial distinction is therefore called for be-tween vocation and occupation. Christians have one vo-cation, though many occupations. Every Christian's vocation is the same, it is the calling to be God's servant in the world. Our occupations, on the other hand, vary— they are jobs, the things we may do as students, stone-masons, accountants, psychologists, auto-parts salesper-sons, or homemakers. The call transcends and transforms them all, and makes occupations arenas in which we hear and fulfill our call in fellowship with Christ.

Organ of faith

So we must pray, for a call depends on hearing a Voice. The organ of faith is the ear, not the eye; we walk by faith, not by sight. First and last, a call is something one listens for. Everything depends on the relationship of the listener to the One who calls.

It's like the tale of a father and a son on a journey to a distant city. There were no maps. The trip would be long and hard, fraught with danger. Only the wisdom and experience of the father would get them safely to their destination. Along the way the boy grew curious about his surroundings. What was on the other side of the forest? What would he see if he stood on that distant ridge? Could he run over there and look? His father said yes.

But the boy was a little nervous. "What if I wander too far from you, Father? What if I get lost?"

The father said, "Every few minutes I will call your name and wait for your answer. Listen for my voice, my son. When you can no longer hear me you will know you've gone too far."

Everything depends on the relationship of the listener to the One who calls. God called Abraham to go to a land that "I will show you" (Gen. 12:1). Why didn't God just tell Abraham where he wanted him to go, give him what he needed to get there, and be done with it, then and there? Why this "I will show you" business? It's so frustrating! But God knows us too well. He knows that if we had the plan and the place, we'd try to get there without him. Just ask Abraham. And we need God far more than we need the plan and the place. Though severe, it's a mercy when he lets us grow weary and dry up inside. For then we come back to him. Just ask Abraham.

That's why we pray. And that's why we get so exhausted when we don't. For when we lose him who is the Way we lose the way.

> What a friend we have in Jesus,
> All our sins and griefs to bear;
> What a privilege to carry
> Everything to God in prayer!
> O what peace we often forfeit,
> O what needless pain we bear,
> All because we do not carry
> Everything to God in prayer.
> Are we weak and heavy laden,
> Cumbered with a load of care?
> Precious Savior, still our refuge;
> Take it to the Lord in prayer.
> Do thy friends despise, forsake thee?
> Take it to the Lord in prayer;
> In His arms he'll take and shield thee,
> Thou wilt find a solace there.[5]

Amen.

---

[5]Joseph Scriven, Charles C. Converse, "What a Friend We Have in Jesus," in *Hymns*, Paul Beckwith, ed. (Chicago: InterVarsity Press, 1952), No. 111.

4

HOLY GREED

I WAS ON MY WAY TO EAT at a friend's house, a gourmet cook of the nouvelle cuisine persuasion—she made exquisitely great food, beautifully presented, but usually not enough for my appetite. Those delicious little servings mocked me. I had missed lunch that day and was ravenous as I made my way to her new address. There was something missing in the directions and I was having a hard time finding her house.

As I drove around, famished and lost, I kept driving by a fast-food restaurant that specialized in hot dogs. The aroma emanating from the drive-thru food trough was having the same effect the sirens of the Greek myth had on the hapless sailors who sailed into their waters. *I don't merely want a hot dog, I need a hot dog,* I reasoned. *She never serves enough food anyway. Why not have just a little snack to hold me over until I find her house?*

I stopped to order a snack. But what to order? The menu was huge. After a panicky exchange with the disembodied voice from the speaker in the drive-thru, I settled on a regular hot dog, a kraut dog, and a chili dog. The hot dogs really aren't very big. And what's a hot dog without French fries?—a day without the sun, oatmeal raisin cookies without cold milk! So I ordered a large fries to cover the demands of the three hot dogs. Fries are salty and hot dogs are spicy, so I added a large soft drink to wash all this down. I felt much better.

When I finally found her house, she had prepared a wonderful meal. It was probably the best meal I didn't enjoy. I was so full, I even left food on the little plates.

A parable of prayer, this silly but true story. Or rather, a parable of prayerlessness. Why don't we pray? We don't pray for the same reason I couldn't enjoy that gourmet meal; we're stuffed in our spirits, full, over-loaded, packed, soul-crammed—not with the Bread of Life, but with spiritual junk food. Before it is anything else, lack of prayer is a lack of hunger for God.

Too easily pleased

Does God think we want too much or too little out of life? What is his chief complaint with us? Let's look at what C. S. Lewis has to say about it:

> [If] we consider the unblushing promises of reward and the staggering nature of the rewards promised in the Gospels, it would seem that our Lord finds our desires not too strong, but too weak. We are half-hearted creatures, fooling about with drink and sex and ambition when infinite joy is offered us, like an ignorant child who wants to go on making mud pies in a slum because he cannot imagine what is meant by the offer of a holiday at the sea. We are far too easily pleased.[1]

[1]C. S. Lewis, *The Weight of Glory* (New York: The Macmillan Company, 1949), 1–2.

That last line is the answer: "We are far too easily pleased." Our desires are not too strong, they're too weak. That, I believe, is God's chief complaint with his people. To add insult to injury, it seems that most Christians tend to think the opposite of God. They see him as a kind of nouvelle cuisine chef, pretty good but stingy.

Just how upset is the Lord about all this? He says it is cause for even the heavens to " 'be appalled . . . and shudder with great horror.' " As he describes it to Jeremiah, " 'My people have committed two sins: They have forsaken me, the spring of living water, and have dug their own cisterns, broken cisterns that cannot hold water' " (2:12–13). They prefer no water to living water, less over more. Mere drink, sex, and ambition outdraw infinite joy! Go figure.

Filling our bellies

Broken cisterns are idols, God-substitutes. They are the spiritual hot dogs we ingest on the way to God's banquet. They dull and eventually kill our appetite for the deep and nourishing richness of his holy fare. Like the Turkish delight the witch gives to Edmund in C. S. Lewis's *The Lion, the Witch, and the Wardrobe*, they are insatiably unsatisfying.[2] The more we eat, the less we like what we eat, but the more we want to eat it. So Frederick Buechner defines gluttony as raiding the refrigerator to cure a case of spiritual malnutrition; and lust as the craving for salt of a man dying of thirst.[3]

Broken cisterns can even be legitimate hungers, like the craving for food of people who are genuinely hungry. After Jesus miraculously fed the multitudes by the lake, they

---

[2]C. S. Lewis, *The Lion, the Witch, and the Wardrobe* (New York: HarperCollins, 1994).
[3]Frederick Buechner, *Wishful Thinking* (New York: Harper & Row, 1973), 31, 54.

wanted to make him king. So he escaped to the other side of the lake. They followed him there, too. When they found him, he confronted them with words that one doesn't speak lightly to folks living in what we would today call a Third World country. He said, " 'I tell you the truth, you are looking for me, not because you saw miraculous signs but because you ate the loaves and had your fill. Do not work for food that spoils, but for food that endures to eternal life, which the Son of Man will give you' " (John 6:26–27). Jesus speaks harshly, for the Greek word translated "had your fill" is a word that is used of animals filling their bellies. He takes a dim view even of a legitimate appetite if it dulls one's hunger for more important things.

Contrast their appetite with King David's, who was in a real desert and was really hungry and really thirsty. But he knew his physical hunger pointed to something eternal and deeper than mere food. It was a signpost to God. He wrote:

> O God, you are my God,
>   earnestly I seek you;
> my soul thirsts for you,
>   my body longs for you,
> in a dry and weary land
>   where there is no water. . . .
> Because your love is better than life,
>   my lips will glorify you.
> I will praise you as long as I live,
>   and in your name I will lift up my hands.
> My soul will be satisfied as with the
>   richest of foods. (Ps. 63:1, 3–5)

We can fill our bellies with things other than mere drink, sex, and ambition. They could be mere work or entertainment. Or mere church. It happens when we let the routines of church attendance and religious activities crowd out living and longing for the kingdom and glory of God. The disappointment and exhaustion of ecclesiastical exertions—of endless meetings and gatherings and committees and programs—can dull our appetite for God. Quietly, imperceptibly, we begin to expect less of him, and end up being satisfied with that. Good church people can stop wondering. *Why was it that wherever Paul went people rioted, but wherever we meet, they serve coffee?*

But over time, we sigh with the chap who wrote, "My cry used to be, 'Win the world for Christ.' Now it's 'Try not to lose too many.'" The church can be so very, very dull and dulling. And those active in it can become the same.

Not that there is anything wrong with the dull. Brother Lawrence spied the glory and presence of God amid the dirty pots and pans of a monastery kitchen. That is the point. He wasn't satisfied with the dull. He was still hungry and thirsty for righteousness. He insisted on looking for glory in the dull, on serving God in the mundane. So he prayed as he scrubbed and scrubbed as he prayed, believing with Irenaeus that the "glory of God is man fully alive, and the life of man is the vision of God." He would settle for no less than to meet face-to-face with the living God, even if it was over a kitchen sink. If he could search for God and find him amid pots and pans, is it too much to pray that we do the same in the dulling routines of life in our time?

We must pray that God will give us the same holy hunger and greed for God! We must look for his glory in the mundane of mere "churchness." We must demand that we find it. We must wrestle with God, as Jacob wrestled with the angel, refusing to let go of him until he blesses us.

Restoring the hunger

Two things have helped me restore my spiritual hunger. The first is simply to memorize some of the hungry, ravenous, visionary prayers of Scripture. Paul's prayers are especially good for this. Take, for example, his prayer for the Ephesians, that "the eyes of your heart may be enlightened in order that you may know the hope to which he has called you, the riches of his glorious inheritance in the saints" (1:18). Or, "that you may be filled to the measure of all the fullness of God" (3:19).

The thought of memorizing prayers seems an artificial and stilted way to restore something as vital as spiritual hunger. But consider what Rabbi Abraham Heschel said to the members of his synagogue who complained that the words of the liturgy did not express what they felt. He told them that it was not that the liturgy should express what they feel, but that they should learn to feel what the liturgy expressed. Recited faithfully, great thoughts put into great words can do that for us. True, God's way to change us is to first change our hearts, working from the inside out. But paradoxically, sometimes the route he takes to our hearts can be to work from the outside in. Memorization can be to our hunger for God what practicing a musical instrument is for performance. It can be the singing of the scales of the soul.

So learn these prayers, these hungry, visionary prayers of Scripture and the great saints—the distilled wisdom of the church. Say them as you step into a board meeting or face a pile of unanswered correspondence. Recite them as you go through your telephone messages and as you drive to the hospital. And if the prayers don't express what you feel, pray them until you feel what they express. Settle for nothing less than the measure of all the fullness of God.

Another way to restore your hunger for God is to choose hunger of another kind—to engage in the ancient practice of fasting. I have only recently, and with great reluctance, walked on this path toward spiritual hunger—

actually, stumbled onto it is a better way to describe it. I'd like to tell you about it.

Someone said the prospect of standing before a firing squad marvelously focuses one's mind. Other things can have the same effect: for instance, the telephone call from a friend of mine last March in which he told me he thought perhaps the Lord was leading us to fast for forty days. Us? I hate to fast. My previous experience of fasting had left me feeling like the man my dad joked about who hit himself over the head with a hammer because it felt so good when he stopped. Even liver and onions would have hit the spot when I broke the fast.

But I don't think that's what the Lord Jesus was shooting for when he set out on his forty-day experience in the wilderness.

The benefits and meaning of fasting had eluded me. I'd tried it before, but instead of insights I got irritable. No, I got nasty. When Bill Bright reported on his forty-day fast, I held him in awe, but with the same detached awe I have for a man who can run a mile under four minutes. It's amazing that he can do it, but it would be futile for me to even try.

So my friend's call got my attention. I trust him, so if he thinks the Lord may be saying something to him about what we should do, I'll give it serious consideration. I did, and as I prayed about it, the unwelcome conviction grew in me that a forty-day fast was precisely what God was asking of us. So we covenanted together with about thirty or forty other people to do this for the forty days leading up to Pentecost Sunday. The purpose would be to fast and pray for the two things Jonathan Edwards urged the churches of eighteenth-century New England to pray for: the spiritual awakening of the church in our town and beyond, and the spread of the kingdom of God worldwide.

The mode of the fast would vary from person to person. Some would take only juices. My wife and I would do a "Daniel" fast and eat only fruits, vegetables, and grains— no meats, fats, or sugar. From time to time during the fast, as the Lord led, we too would have a day of juice only. Also, whenever possible, all of us who had covenanted to fast would meet for an hour of prayer on Friday mornings.

From command to permission

The fast ended, I lost about twenty-five pounds, and while it remains to be seen exactly what our prayer and fasting will mean for the wider kingdom of God, my mind has been marvelously focused in a few important ways. The first is what a slave I can be to food. Food and its consumption is omnipresent in my life. It is the all-purpose elixir. Am I sad? Eat. Am I happy? Eat. Tired? Eat. Angry, depressed, bored? Eat, eat, eat. Do we have a social occasion? We must eat. Do we have a meeting to discuss business? We should eat. And on and on and on. I must have food. My life can be a parody of 1 Thessalonians 5:16–18. "Be [eating] always, [eat] continually; [eat] in all circumstances." I'm exaggerating, but I can see possibilities for the enjoyment of food at every turn.

Your food may be your addiction to work or to sex or to entertainment. I am convinced that for much of the church in North America, it is our addiction to the busyness of programs and church activities.

I was surprised, then exhilarated, at how free I was during the fast. To my delight, I discovered that what I decided I must not do for a season was also something that I may not do. What began as a command quickly became a permission. The permission? Not to have to live on the level of my appetites. We must eat to live, God made us that way.

But he made us for more than food, he made us for himself. And if we glom on to his gifts so that we lose sight of the Giver, we become not only idolaters but slaves, and we starve spiritually.

That brings us back to those broken cisterns—the God-substitutes, the craving for salt of a man dying of thirst. It's what Jesus said to the hungry crowd: "Do not work for food that spoils, but for food that endures to eternal life, which the Son of Man will give you" (John 6:27). The saying "You are what you eat" is true in more ways than one.

Because of this, it soon became apparent to me that ending the fast would be as important as beginning it. For as the fast came to an end, I actually became a little nervous, almost afraid to go back to eating normally, for fear I might lose the new freedom I had gained—lose it with the freedom to eat more varieties of food.

Second, my mind was marvelously focused on the fact that gluttony is about more than mere volume of food. It can also express itself as an inordinate interest in the *experience* of food, making taste buds promiscuous and stomachs ravenous for novelty and variety. I eat out often, and one of my occupational hazards comes through the increasingly voluminous pages of menus I open in restaurants. Some read like travelogues, describing the exotic, even spiritual experiences I will have if I order this item or that. I've seen chocolate desserts described as "pure sin" and roast beef and mashed potatoes as "comfort."

The fast focused my mind on the simple goodness of God's creation. At first, the foods I restricted myself to made the prospect of a meal seem a boring event. Beans again? Another salad? But soon I rediscovered just how good a mere carrot can taste. A carrot, nothing more. Or a plain slice of bread, or a crisp apple. With simplicity comes gratitude and joy.

Blessed are the hungry

The third and most marvelous focus the fast brought to my mind was that food is ultimately not about food but about God. This is also true with all other appetites and longings, be they ambition or companionship or success or sex. The meaning of hunger, indeed of all desire, is to point us to God. It can be a good thing to be hungry. We shouldn't be too quick to make it go away, for it can teach us much about our frailty, need, and ultimate emptiness and despair apart from God. Dissatisfaction and discontent, longing and restlessness can be marvelous tutors.

The seventeenth-century pastor and poet George Herbert pictured God pouring every blessing into his human creature—beauty, wisdom, honor, pleasure—but stopping when it came to the blessing of rest or satisfaction. Herbert reasoned that if God bestowed rest along with all his other blessings, man would remember God's gifts instead of God himself:

> He would adore My gifts instead of me,
> And rest in Nature, not the God of Nature. . . .[4]

God decided it would be better for us to be rich, yet weary and hungry:

> If goodness leade him not, yet weariness
> May tosse him to My breast.[5]

A full stomach can be cause for deep gratitude, or as it has so often been the case for me, cause for spiritual dullness and torpor. A little hunger never hurt anyone, but its

---

[4]George Herbert, "The Pulley," (New York: AMS Press, The Fuller Worthies Library, 1874), 183.
[5]Ibid., 184.

absence might. We are more than our stomach, much, much more. We may never know this until we let it ache.

Perfect Host

What's your image of God? The Bible portrays him as King, Warrior, Husband, and above all, as the Father of the Lord Jesus Christ. Have you ever thought of him as a host? When the Prodigal Son came home, his father threw a big barbecue to celebrate his return. Jesus said God is like that. Can you picture him dressed in black pinstripe pants and a red brocade vest, face beaming with delight as he fills the glasses of his guests?

He showed himself that way to the prophet Isaiah:

"Come, all you who are thirsty,
    come to the waters;
and you who have no money,
    come, buy and eat!
Come, buy wine and milk
    without money and without cost.
Why spend money on what is not bread,
    and your labor on what
    does not satisfy?
Listen, listen to me, and eat
    what is good,
    and your soul will delight
    in the richest of fare.
Give ear and come to me;
    hear me, that your soul may live."
                    (Isa. 55:1–3)

There's pleading in those words. God wants us to come and eat and be satisfied in him. Can you see him humbling himself, even leaving the party, and going outside to plead with the son who won't feast? Begging him to come inside and eat and be joyful in the joy of his father? He's still doing that with his prayerless people.

5

THE PLEASURE OF HIS COMPANY

I HATE TO FLY. But since I fly a lot, I have developed several techniques to steel myself against the cramped seating, the stale air, and the terrors of turbulence. Escapist reading material and a tape player with a headset do nicely. The overall desired effect is to implode into myself until I get off the plane. For this reason I rarely engage in conversation in flight. Besides, the effort involved in looking at a seatmate gives me a crick in my neck. If I want to ward off a gregarious fellow traveler, I open my Bible in my lap.

Such was my mood as I sat awaiting a flight in the John Wayne Airport in Orange County, California. So I was dimly aware of the well-dressed couple standing in front of me. Each was shouldering a large leather attaché bag, fumbling with papers and tickets inside and chattering to the other. I guessed them to be attorneys. Maybe it was the tasseled loafers the man was wearing.

In the middle of the conversation, a strange thing happened. The woman puckered her lips and moved to kiss the man. She came within mere inches of his face, only to realize that he wasn't aware of her intentions. He just kept on fumbling with the contents of his bag, talking to her but not looking at her as he did. She unpuckered and withdrew to her bag and chatter.

They had my attention. I laid my book aside and took off my headset to watch this little drama. Then something even stranger happened. The man stopped fumbling in his bag, puckered up his lips and moved to kiss her, came to within inches of her face, only to discover that she didn't notice what he was attempting. He chickened out. It was now his turn to go back to his bag and chatter.

I was on the edge of my seat mentally as the dance became stranger still. She again puckered, moved to kiss him, came within a breath of his face, saw that he was oblivious to her intentions, and withdrew again. Then he did the same thing, again! I was on the verge of getting up and offering my services as a pastoral counselor, when one of the flights was called and they parted.

It occurred to me then, and still does, that whatever else they may have accomplished that day, they had already missed the most important thing they could have done. They may have negotiated multimillion dollar deals, but no matter—they hadn't kissed. The day had already been wasted.

I take this story as a parable of the gift of prayer—and our struggle with that gift.

How personal is God?

Hold that picture in mind, and hear the desire of Christ. He says, "Here I am! I stand at the door and knock. If anyone hears my voice and opens the door, I will come in and eat with him, and he with me" (Rev. 3:20). Almighty God, the Lord of Eternity, wants to be intimate with us, to draw near and spend time with us. He holds out a tender, wonderful, *incredible* offering. But we, like the couple at the airport, are so blind, so preoccupied, that we miss the invitation. Not only does God command us to pray, he *permits* us to pray. Prayer is both a must and a *may*, an obligation and a *gift*. Why would any of us ignore the God of the universe, bending low to offer us the pleasure of his company?

One reason may be simple ignorance—we do not really understand just how personal this God is. We have the intellectuals, among others, to thank for this. These are the folks who gave us god as the "Principle of Concretion" (Alfred North Whitehead); or the "Integrating Factor in Experience" (Henry Nelson Wieman); or "The Ground of All Being" (Paul Tillich). Entertainers, too, have served up this vapid deity, as in George Lucas's "the force" in the *Star Wars* films. The God they describe is an elitist deity; so distant he cannot be approached unless you think you're smart enough to understand whatever a principle of concretion is.

That may be the point of these false gods—to keep them distant. Have you heard the one about the theologian who, given the choice between going to heaven or hearing a lecture about heaven, chose the lecture? *Confine God to the cerebral cortex and he won't be able to mess up your plans.* The more abstract and impersonal you can make him, the less demanding he will be. Thus spiritual avoidance poses as intellectual depth.

Safe, boring, and shrunken

But the God Jesus tells us to pray to is not the God of the philosophers and pantheists. In a brilliant section in his book *Miracles*, C. S. Lewis exposed the bogus appeal of the impersonal God:

Men are reluctant to pass over from the notion of an abstract and negative deity to the living God. I do not wonder. Here lies the deepest tap-root of Pantheism and of the objection to traditional imagery. It was hated not, at bottom, because it pictured him as man but because it pictured him as king, or even as warrior. The Pantheist's God does nothing, demands nothing. He is there if you wish for him, like a book on a shelf. He will not pursue you. There is no danger that at any time heaven and earth should flee away at his glance. If he were the truth, then we could really say that all the Christian images of kingship were a historical accident of which our religion ought to be cleansed.

It is with a shock that we discover them to be indispensable. You have had a shock like that before, in connection with smaller matters—when the line pulls at your hand, when something breathes beside you in the darkness. So here; the shock comes at the precise moment when the thrill of *life* is communicated to us along the clue we have been following. It is always shocking to meet life where we thought we were alone. "Look out!" we cry, "it's *alive*." And therefore this is the very point at which so many draw back—I would have done so myself if I could—and proceed no further with Christianity. An "impersonal God"—well and good. A subjective God of beauty, truth, and goodness, inside our own heads—better still. A formless life-force surging through us, a vast power which we can tap—best of all. But God himself, alive, pulling at the other end of the cord, perhaps approaching at an infinite speed, the hunter, King, husband—that is quite another matter. Here comes a moment when the children who have been playing at burglars hush suddenly: was that a *real* footstep in the hall? There comes a moment when people who have been dabbling in religion ("man's search for God") suddenly draw back. Supposing we really found him? We never meant it to come to *that*! Worse still, supposing he had found us?[1]

The less demanding and personal God is, the more boring he will be. One doesn't pray to a God like that, one meditates; except for an elite few, one loses interest and falls asleep. An abstract, boring God is finally a shrunken God, too big and therefore too busy, we think, to get involved with people. But the God Jesus told us to pray to can both run the cosmos and knit a baby together in his mother's womb. He can number both subatomic particles and the hairs on your head. Anything less, and he is shrunk to the size of the senator Julia Ward Howe invited to her home. She wanted him to meet the up-and-coming actor Edwin Booth, but he declined, explaining loftily, "The truth is, I have got beyond taking an interest in individuals." She later commented sarcastically on his remark in her diary: "God Almighty has not got so far."

Indeed, George Buttrick was right when he said, "The field of second-rate religion is strewn with the corpses of abstract nouns." A second-rate God will elicit a second-rate, boring prayer life.

Fire!

Blaise Pascal had a kind of born-again experience the night of November 23, 1654. A brilliant scientist and intellectual, Pascal met God, as it were, face to face, and wrote what he saw and felt, as it was happening to him. He

---

[1]C. S. Lewis, *Miracles* (New York: Touchstone, 1996), 124–25.

recorded on a piece of parchment, "From about half past ten in the evening until half past midnight."

A scientist would want to remember the exact time. The piece of parchment was sewn in his coat and found after his death. It seems that he carried it with him continually. The first word he used to describe the experience was simply "fire." That alone set the personal God he met apart from the impersonal god of mere intellect and ideas. The next sentence is more telling: "God of Abraham, God of Isaac, God of Jacob, *not of philosophers and scholars*" (italics mine). His experience is a model of what it means to pray to the personal God of the Bible. His prayer is not Scripture, but it is scriptural in its stream-of-consciousness fervor.

> Certainty, certainty,
> heartfelt, joy, peace.
> God of Jesus Christ.
> God of Jesus Christ.
> *My God and your God.*
> "Thy God shall be my God."
> The world forgotten,
> and everything except God.
> He can only be found by ways
> taught in the Gospels.
> Greatness of the human soul.
> "O righteous Father,
> the world has not known thee,
> but I have known thee."
> Joy, joy, joy, tears of joy.
> I have cut myself off from him.
> *They have forsaken me,*
> *the fountain of living waters.*
> My God, wilt thou forsake me?
> Let me not be cut off from him forever!

"And this is life eternal,
that they may know thee,
the only true God,
and Jesus Christ whom thou hast sent."
Jesus Christ
Jesus Christ
I have cut myself off from him,
shunned him, denied him, crucified him.
Let me never be cut off from him!
He can only be kept
by the ways taught in the Gospel.
Sweet and total renunciation.
Total submission to Jesus Christ
and my director.
Everlasting joy
in return for one day's effort
on earth.
I will not forget thy word.
Amen.[2]

We all long to meet an awesome and personal God like that in prayer.

In fear of Abba

Jesus said to address this awesome God as *Abba*, Aramaic for "dear Father," or "Daddy." He said if you can understand how a good human father operates, then you will understand a little of what God is like. "Which of you [fathers], if his son asks for bread, will give him a stone? Or if he asks for a fish, will give him a snake? If you, then, though you are evil, know how to give good gifts to your children, how much more will your Father in heaven give

---

[2]Blaise Pascal, *Pensées*, A. J. Krailsheimer, trans. (New York: Penguin Books, 1983).

good gifts to those who ask him!" (Matt. 7:9–11).

Call God *Abba*. Pray to him as Daddy. That alone can make your prayers burst into significance. The Heidelberg Catechism asks, "Why has Christ commanded us to address God as 'Our Father'?" It answers, "That immediately, at the beginning of our prayer, he might excite in us a childlike reverence for, and confidence in, God, which are the *foundations of prayer*" (italics mine).[3] St. Teresa of Avila confessed that she found it hard to get beyond the first words in the Lord's Prayer: "Our Father." For her they were like a lovely land she never wanted to leave.

But my experience has often been that the very words that should excite such reverence and delight in prayer can produce the opposite effect. "Father" can become a household word in the sense of pots and pans and dull, unconscious routines. We can begin to speak it as we would at the dinner table: "Hey, Dad, pass the salt." Or use it as punctuation, not much more than a comma, on our prayers: "Father, we just want you to bless us, Father, because, Father, you know our needs, Father."

Before that word "Father" can ignite in us all the wonder and adoration Jesus meant it to, we must first appreciate something else about God, something many of us think to be at odds with addressing him as Father. It is that our Father God is awesome and holy, terrible in power, breathtaking in wisdom. He is one to be *feared*. The Bible is full of this fear language, commanding it, even celebrating it.

> Serve the Lord with fear
>   and rejoice with trembling. (Ps. 2:11)

---

[3]Heidelberg Catechism, Question 120 (Phillipsburg, N. J.: Presbyterian and Reformed Publishing Company, reproduction of the Second American Edition, printed in Columbus, Ohio, 1852), 626.

Let all the earth fear the Lord;
    let all the people of the world
    revere him. (Ps. 33:8)
The fear of the Lord is the beginning
    of knowledge. (Prov. 1:7)
Now all has been heard;
    here is the conclusion of the matter:
Fear God and keep his
    commandments,
    for this is the *whole duty of man*.
        (Eccles. 12:13, italics mine)
Since, then, we know what it is to fear the Lord,
    we try to persuade men. (2 Cor. 5:11)
Work out your salvation with fear and trembling.
    (Phil. 2:12)

What does it mean to fear God? Does it mean to fear him as we would a poisonous snake or a blood transfusion tainted with the HIV virus? We know it doesn't, but we're not sure why.

The words the Bible uses mean literally "to fear." Translators try alternatives, words like *awe, respect, reverence,* but none quite captures the raw strength of the word *fear.* The key to what the Bible means lies, I think, in what happens to our consciousness when we fear something. As I said earlier, someone once said that standing before a firing squad marvelously focuses one's mind. The idea is that the experience of being brought right up to the point of death, and then given a reprieve, brings focus. That's the key: *What we fear marvelously focuses us.* The fear of God is respect and awe and reverence. But it is these things, to a degree, that are *like terror in their intensity.*

Therefore, the Bible sees no conflict between fearing God and loving and trusting him. Amazingly, when Jesus wants to calm our fears, he tells us to first fear God!

75

" 'I tell you, my friends, do not be afraid of those who kill the body and after that can do no more. But I will show you whom you should fear: Fear him who, after the killing of the body, has power to throw you into hell. Yes, I tell you, fear him' " (Luke 12:4–5).

That's God he's talking about, the one who can throw us into hell, *and* the one we are to address in prayer as *Abba*, Daddy. Then, without even a break or segue in thought, he says we should relax: " 'Indeed, the very hairs of your head are all numbered. Don't be afraid; you are worth more than many sparrows' " (v. 7). His message: You are worth everything to the One who is to be feared. *Fear God and you'll fear nothing else!*

Later, in the same chapter, Jesus utters some of my favorite words: " 'Do not be afraid, little flock, for your Father has been pleased to give you the kingdom' " (Luke 12:32).

Jabba the Butt

What one most deeply loves, one most deeply fears. My wife, Lauretta, is the dearest person I know, and apart from Jesus, the clearest, most incontrovertible evidence of God's grace to me. At its best, my love for her is like terror in its intensity. Oh, the fear I have of hurting her! Her worth is staggering in its weight.

Then there are my children. On the night our first child was born, I remember washing up to go into the delivery room to accompany Lauretta in his birth. I say "accompany," the Lamaze teacher said it was to "assist." But after watching the holy ordeal of childbirth, I decided I could be of no real assistance. As I washed, a terror came over me. This was *it*. Things were going to change for me for the rest of my life. The fear and joy of who was about to arrive nearly bowled me over. Could I care for him adequately? Could I really be a father? Somehow I had a fear of holding him and dropping him. And then, minutes later, there I stood in the gleaming room holding him, trembling with love and fear. Though less than eight pounds, his worth was staggering in its weight.

Later, when more children came, and they got old enough to wrestle with me, we would play a game we called "Jabba the Butt." The name came from a large, disgusting evil character in the *Star Wars* trilogy called Jabba the Hutt. We changed the surname for the sake of humor. I would play Jabba and roar around the room as the kids would shoot their laser guns at me and try to wrestle me to the floor. Sometimes I would get into the role too much and their little imaginations would slip into stark terror. They would feel my great strength and hear my booming voice, and Daddy would be transformed into Jabba. The game would stop, and I would hold them tenderly and remind them that I was their daddy. The juxtaposition of great, overwhelming strength and power with tender love is as hard for a child to hold together as it is for an adult. My love for them was staggering when they coupled it with my power.

Addressing God as Father can become electrifying, if we can put these two together in our minds: combining infinite love and tenderness with infinite holiness and power. It can become the source of our greatest seriousness and our deepest joy, that one of such might can be called Father, and that our Father can be one with such might! He is not like Jabba in evil, but he is in strength. Fear and love go together. To paraphrase Peter Kreeft, the wonder of praying to God as Father can come only when we have learned what seems to be its opposite, that he is the totally Other, the transcendent Creator of time and space, fierce in holiness, awesome in power. If the fear of God is the beginning of wisdom, then filial intimacy is its fulfillment.

"My God, How Wonderful Thou Art"

In hymnody, one of the best treatments of this glorious and holy tension is Frederick Faber's "My God, How Wonderful Thou Art." The hymn begins with a series of exclamations on the fearful worth of God, the brightness of his majesty, the fire of his light, his unbearable beauty. Even the best and brightest of all creation can do no more than fall down before him.

> My God, how wonderful Thou art,
> Thy majesty how bright!
> How beautiful Thy mercy seat,
> In depths of burning light!
> How dread are Thine eternal years,
> O everlasting Lord,
> By prostrate spirits day and night
> Incessantly adored!

What can one do when confronted with such a God, but become marvelously focused? It is the most inexorable of spiritual reflexes. There is really no choice but to be afraid, to experience an awe that is like terror in its intensity.

> O how I fear Thee, living God,
> With deepest, tenderest fears.
> And worship Thee with trembling hope
> And penitential tears!

But then wonder piles upon wonder when a God such as this offers us the pleasure of his company. He wants communion with us. He calls us to prayer! Can it be? Can it really be?

> Yet I may love Thee, too,
> O Lord, Almighty as Thou art,
> For Thou hast stooped to ask of me
> The love of my poor heart.[4]

We can never be too smitten by this. Sometimes I think our hands are cauterized by too much handling of holy things. Our hearts get calluses. Liturgical traditions are susceptible to worshipers who declare the burning realities in a singsong voice. I've heard the *Te Deum* read like a recipe for chocolate cake. So-called nonliturgical traditions fall prey to the trite and the garrulous. I think it must have been something like that that led humorist Roy Blount to wonder if anyone is concerned that they may be boring God. No character in the Bible found anything approaching a face-to-face encounter with God anything less than shattering. We must learn to act and think as people who are amazed that our proximity to holy things has not left us vaporized. We must pray that God will cultivate in our spirits fresh awareness of his majesty and goodness, and that we not confuse his goodness with his being safe. Like the lion Aslan in C. S. Lewis's *The Lion, the Witch, and the Wardrobe*, "He isn't safe. But he's good." God being God, Annie Dillard playfully suggested that we should wear crash helmets when we worship.

I have taken to reading these lines from Ecclesiastes before I go to a worship service:

> Guard your steps when you go to the house of God.
> Go near to listen rather than to offer the sacrifice
> of fools, who do not know that they do wrong.

---

[4]Frederick Faber, "My God, How Wonderful Thou Art," *Hymns of the Christian Life* (Harrisburg, Pa.: Christian Publications, Inc., 1962), No. 17.

Do not be quick with your mouth,
>   do not be hasty in your heart
>   to utter anything before God.
> God is in heaven
>   and you are on earth,
>   so let your words be few.
> As a dream comes when there are
>   many cares,
>   so the speech of a fool when there are
>   many words. . . .
> Therefore stand in awe of God. (Eccles. 5:1–3, 7)

Yada, yada, yada

We may pray because God is personal; he wants to be *known*. There is another, equally transforming side to this breathtaking reality: we may pray because *he knows us*. His knowledge is not the knowledge of an immense, passive intellect, but of intimate, transforming contact, as in when "Adam *knew* his wife Eve, and she conceived" (Gen. 4:1 NRSV). The Hebrew word for this knowledge, *yada*, can mean the knowledge of transformation or of understanding, depending on its context. But it is commonly used of the kind of intimate, sexual knowledge that Adam clearly had of Eve when she became pregnant.

Yada, to know—it's surprising the Bible uses a word like this to speak of something that we typically describe more clinically as "having sex," or perhaps more euphemistically as "having relations." Modern translations render this verse with such words as "lay" (New International Version), "had relations" (New American Standard), "slept" (New Living Translation), "had intercourse" (Jerusalem Bible). But the Hebrew text says Adam *knew* Eve, and she conceived a child, a new life.

God's knowledge of us is like that. That is not to say that his knowledge of us is sexual, but sexual knowledge is something like his knowledge of us. It is deeply intimate, life-creating, in-fleshed, and therefore transforming. Thomas Howard calls this a "piquant irony":

> [Here] we are, with all of our high notions of ourselves as intellectual and spiritual beings, and the most profound form of knowledge for us is a plain business of skin on skin. It is humiliating. When two members of this godlike, cerebral species approach the heights of communion between themselves, what do they do? Think? Speculate? Meditate? No, they take off their clothes. Do they want to get their *brains* together? No. It is the most appalling of ironies: their search for union takes them quite literally in a direction away from where their brains are.[5]

Howard asks, what is the meaning of all this? It has to do with the fact that true knowledge of the other is much more than amassing data about that person. It must be increasingly synonymous with Love, that is, with self-giving, mutuality, and union, as we press further and further in towards the center.

Naturally King David is amazed and *impregnated*, as it were, with hope and delight, when he realizes that he is *known* by God:

> O Lord, you have searched me
>   and you know me.
> You know when I sit and when I rise;
>   you perceive my thoughts from afar.

---

[5]Thomas Howard, *Hallowed by This House* (San Francisco: Ignatius Press, 1979), 115–17.

> You discern my going out and my
>> lying down;
>> you are familiar with all my ways.
> Before a word is on my tongue
>> you know it completely, O Lord. . . .
> For you created my inmost being;
>> you knit me together in my
>> mother's womb. (Ps. 139:1–4, 13)

To know something is good, even great. To be known is transforming.

I was in college the first time I truly felt known and loved by God. I was walking back to my dorm, and suddenly it came to me that God knew me intimately. It was a shattering, wonderful feeling. *God knows me*, I thought. *He really loves me.* At the time I had a great roommate, and he and a bunch of other guys and I would sit around until all hours of the night talking. It would get late, and we would get just tired enough to let our guard come down. Then one of us would let slip some revelation about his innermost self. He would feel embarrassed, until someone looked at him and said, "You too?" He knew—and he was known. Somehow, being in that position of vulnerability and sympathetic intimacy opened me up to the sense of God's deep and close knowing of me. In those late night conversations I was impregnated with a new life that has grown in me ever since. It's wonderful to know. It is more wonderful to be known.

In April 1995, we experienced a student revival on our campus that dramatically illustrated the power of feeling known by God. In a chapel service, students began to spontaneously confess their sins in public! Students streamed up to the microphone, openly speaking of their sins and struggles. Short of murder, I can't think of a sin that wasn't confessed or a struggle that wasn't shared. Rape, incest, drug abuse, eating disorders—all were aired in front of hundreds of people. Each student would speak, walk away from the microphone, and be surrounded by friends. Hugs, tears, and prayers of encouragement and healing would follow. This went on for several nights.

These young people had been told a lie their whole lives, a lie that said, "You're alone in your struggles. No one knows you." That's a terrible feeling with which to live. They longed to be known—don't we all?—but at the same time, it's terrifying to lay oneself bare before others. The Spirit moved among those students to give them the gift of being known. He empowered them to discover, finally, that to be completely transparent and to feel completely loved is to come closer to the heart of God. So it is for all of us. The gift of prayer is that we can lay all that we are before God, who won't be surprised or shocked at anything we say.

A week after these experiences at Hope College, I went to Chicago to attend a National Day of Prayer event. Different pastors spoke on what God was doing in their communities. One of them, a pastor from Texas, had a ministry with street gangs, which in itself was amazing, because he didn't look like the kind of man one would think would have that kind of outreach. But he had led the leaders of rival gangs to Christ, and told us a story about baptizing one of the boys. The pastor was going to sprinkle him in church, but the kid wanted to be baptized in the river. He had probably committed murder, and he wanted to do it all the way.

The pastor said that when he looked at the kid's face under the water, he could see his broken nose. When he lifted the boy out of the water, the kid clung to him and wept and wept and wept. After he finally regained his composure, he said to the pastor, "This is only the second time in my life I've ever cried. The first time was the night my dad broke my nose."

Then the pastor said to us, "I baptized him in water, and he baptized me in his tears. And they washed away all that church stuff."

Jump in the river

God invites us to jump into that river and let him cleanse all that "stuff" from our souls, whether it's church stuff or the numbness of isolation and loneliness. The river is the pleasure of his company, the knowledge of God, his of us and ours of him. It is God's "river of delights" (Ps. 36:8). It is the place where we can stand in his presence and know the joy of his presence, the "eternal pleasures" that are at his right hand (Ps. 16:11).

Go back with me to that scene at the airport. See the couple run off to something, empty inside, not knowing why. Now contrast that with the words of Bernard of Clairvaux:

> Jesus, Thou joy of loving hearts,
> Thou fount of life, Thou light of men,
> From the best bliss that life imparts
> We turn unfilled to thee again.[6]

What no bliss in life can impart is what is given in prayer. It is the pleasure of his company.

---

[6]Bernard of Clairvaux, "Jesus, Thou Joy of Loving Hearts," trans. Ray Palmer (Chicago: InterVarsity Press, 1965), 163.

6

GOD'S MIRTH ROARING
IN OUR VEINS

IMAGINE THE MYSTERY and delight of not only hearing but *seeing* the story of Jesus for the first time, almost as an eyewitness.

That's what happened to a primitive tribe in the jungles of East Asia, when missionaries showed them the *Jesus* film. Not only had these people never heard of Jesus, they had never seen a motion picture. Then, all at once, on one un-forgettable evening, they saw it all—the gospel in their own language, visible and real.

Imagine again, then, how it would feel to see for the first time this good man Jesus, who healed the sick and was adored by children, held without trial and beaten by jeering soldiers. As they watched this, the people came unglued. They stood up and began to shout at the cruel men on the screen, demanding this outrage stop. When nothing hap-pened, they attacked the missionary running the projector. Perhaps he was responsible for this injustice! He was forced to stop the film and explain that the story wasn't over yet, that there was more. So they settled back onto the ground, holding their emotions in tenuous check.

Then came the Crucifixion. Again, the people could not hold back. They began to weep and wail with such loud grief that once again the film had to be stopped. Again the missionary tried to calm them, explaining that the story still wasn't over yet, that there was more. So once again they composed themselves and sat down to see what happened next.

Then came the Resurrection. Pandemonium broke out this time, but for a different reason. The gathering had spontaneously erupted into a party. The noise now was of jubilation, and it was deafening. The people were dancing and slapping each other on the back. The missionary again had to shut off the projector. But this time he didn't tell them to calm down and wait for what was next. In a sense, all that was supposed to happen—in the story and in their lives—was happening.

Alive and enlivened

Imagine a worship service in which the liturgy was periodically interrupted because the people were overcome with the enormity and emotion, the sheer weight of the gospel story; and in which the joy and sadness, the *adoration*, appropriate to such an event would simply take over. Like the primitives they would be fulfilling the purpose for which God made us: which is, according to the Westminster Shorter Catechism, "to glorify God and enjoy him forever."

These two go together, to glorify and enjoy. They are nearly one and the same because as C. S. Lewis observes, "Fully to enjoy is to glorify. In commanding us to glorify Him, God is inviting us to enjoy Him."[1] Wonderful things

---

[1] C. S. Lewis, *Reflections on the Psalms* (New York: Harcourt, Brace, Jovanovich, 1964), 97.

happen to us when we do this.

"God's mirth," says Theodore Jennings, "roars in our veins and we are alive and enlivened."[2] The church father Irenaeus put it this way: "The glory of God is man fully alive, and the life of man is the vision of God."[3] It's true, God is never more glorified than when a human being comes fully alive. It's not in sunsets and oceans. It's not in mountain grandeur and stellar blaze. It's in people.

One evening I was sitting on the edge of my favorite place on earth, the Grand Canyon, watching the sun go down. It's a magnificent sight; the changing of the light, the continual slow-motion movement of the shadows is like a visual fugue. One of my sons was with me, and we were rhapsodizing about the majesty, the glory of God manifest in that place, when I noticed his face outlined against the canyon and the sunset. *My dear son, my beloved son*, I thought. Then it struck me: "You know," I said to him, "there's something here that is even more glorious and godlike than this canyon." He looked at me with a frown of disbelief, and said, "What could that possibly be?" I grinned and said, "You."

More than even the Grand Canyon, he showed the glory of God, because it's not of canyons, but only of humans, that God says, "I made them in my image, like me."

So, of course, God is most glorified when those he made in his image become fully alive, all they were created to be. This can happen but one way: through the vision of God. Paul says, "And we, who with unveiled faces all reflect the Lord's glory, are being transformed into his likeness with ever-increasing glory, which comes from the Lord,

---

[2]Theodore Jennings, *Life As Worship: Prayer and Praise in Jesus' Name* (Grand Rapids: Eerdmans, 1982), 90.

[3]Ireneaus, quoted by William Willimon, *The Service of God* (Nashville: Abingdon Press, 1983), 64.

who is the Spirit" (2 Cor. 3:18). God is glorified as we come alive, his mirth roaring in our veins, as we awaken to the vision of God.

Given, not gotten

There was a time when all those commands of God for us to thank and praise him seemed to me to be a little odd. Did he need them to feel better about himself? Was he like the kid I knew in junior high who stood around with his hands in his pockets fishing for compliments? No, God doesn't need our praise—*we* need to give it. For to praise God is to sharpen our soul's vision of his greatness and goodness, and thus to increase *our* soul's greatness and goodness. God doesn't need our thanks and praise to feel better about himself, we need to thank and praise him to be better ourselves. It is a gift to us to give God thanks and praise.

That's why both are so important.

Consider the power of simple thanksgiving. Its genius is its prerequisite: humility, which is essential to a proper relationship to God. Paul asks, "What do you have that you did not receive?" The answer is *nada*, nothing—absolutely nothing whatsoever. Everything we have is a *given*, not a gotten. We enter the world naked, we exit the world naked. All we have in between is on loan. It's humiliating! Precisely. Then the apostle asks, "And if you did receive it, why do you boast as though you did not?" (1 Cor. 4:7). In other words, what grounds do you have for pride? Same answer: *nada*, nothing—absolutely nothing whatsoever. So "gratitude is a species of justice," writes Samuel Johnson, meaning that when we genuinely say thanks to God, we are seeing things as they actually are, and humbly giving credit where credit is due.

To be ungrateful is to see things as they are *not*, to have a perspective that is fundamentally and fatally distorted. Such is the view of the proud, who see all they have and are as a gotten, not a given. That, says C. S. Lewis, is a "completely anti-God state of mind." God is implacably against the proud, utterly hidden from their sight. The logic is simple: "A proud man is always looking down on things and people: and, of course, as long as you are looking down, you cannot see something that is above you."[4]

If pride is the complete anti-God state of mind, grateful prayer is the complete anti-pride state of mind. It's good, very good for the soul.

Indefatigable, defiant joy

Grateful prayer is also a vigorous exercise, producing an indefatigable, even defiant perseverance and joy. Grounded as it is in humility, it is not stymied when circumstances turn sour. It says, "Who am I to complain when I suffer loss, since whatever I lost was never mine to begin with?" Job is Exhibit A in the Bible of what this looks like in practice. When he loses everything he owns and loves, how does he respond? As one who knew all along that what he had was a given, not a gotten. His first act is to *worship* God!

> Then he fell to the ground in worship and said:

> "Naked I came from my mother's
>   womb,
>   and naked I will depart.
> The Lord gave and the Lord has
>   taken away;

---

[4]C. S. Lewis, *Mere Christianity* (New York: Touchstone Books, 1996), 110–11.

may the name of the Lord
be praised." (Job 1:20–21)

True gratitude is unstoppable.

One of the great hymns of gratitude was written by another man with this kind of defiant humility: Martin Rinkart (1586–1649), a pastor in the city of Elenberg in Saxony, during the Thirty Years War. During that horrible time, all the other pastors in the city left, leaving him with 4,500 funerals to conduct, among them his wife's. As the war drew to a close, the city was overrun by the Austrians once and the Swedes twice. The Swedish general levied a heavy tax on the beleaguered people. Rinkart and his congregation pleaded for the general to show mercy, but he refused. Rinkart then turned to his people and said, "Come, my children; we can find no mercy with man—let us take refuge in God." There, before the general, they knelt in prayer.

The general was so moved by what he saw that he relented and lowered the tax to one-twentieth of what it had been.

Martin Rinkart, the man who saw so much grief and endured so much loss, could still say gratitude's defiant "nevertheless," and write the great, "Now Thank We All Our God":

Now thank we all our God
With heart and hands and voices,
Who wondrous things hath done,
In whom His world rejoices;
Who, from our mother's arms,
Hath blessed us on our way
With countless gifts of love,
And still is ours today.
All praise and thanks to God

The Father now be given,
The Son and Holy Ghost,
Supreme in highest heaven;
The one eternal God,
Whom earth and heaven adore;
For thus it was, is now,
And shall be evermore.[5]

The power of humble gratitude to produce such a defiant joy lies in its insight into the nature of things. Only the humble can see the ultimate goodness and joy that lies at the core of creation, the Father's heart that beats beneath the worst of circumstances. Frederick Buechner discovered this one cold, rainy night in Anniston, Alabama.

On an infantry training bivouac, he was in the last place on earth he wanted to be. That year an uncle had committed suicide, revealing a family darkness no one knew what to do with. Buechner had no idea where he really belonged, all he knew was where he didn't want to be: there—eating his supper out of a mess kit. But the grace of gratitude gave him a new vision of things:

> There was a cold drizzle of rain, and everything was mud. The sun had gone down. I was still hungry when I finished and noticed that a man nearby had something left over that he was not going to eat. It was a turnip, and when I asked him if I could have it, he tossed it over to me. I missed the catch, the turnip fell to the ground, but I wanted it so badly that I picked it up and started eating it, mud and all. And then, as I ate it, time deepened and slowed down again. With a lurch of the heart that is real to me still, I saw it suddenly, almost as if from

---

[5]Martin Rinkart, "Now Thank We All Our God," *Hymns II* (Downers Grove, Ill.: InterVarsity Press, 1976), 148.

beyond time all together, that not only was the turnip good, but the mud was good too, even the drizzle and the cold were good, even the Army that I had dreaded for months. Sitting there in the cold Alabama winter with my mouth full of cold turnip and mud, I could see at least for a moment how if you ever took truly to heart the ultimate goodness and joy of things, even at their bleakest, the need to praise someone or something for it would be so great that you might even go out and speak of it to the birds of the air.[6]

Thank therapy

One year when I was on vacation in Minnesota, I dreaded the day when I would have to go back to my church to work. The problems seemed endless and insoluble. I was suffering, my children were suffering, and my wife was worried about us all. When the day came to leave, I loaded everybody up in my van, set my jaw, gritted my teeth, and headed home, grimly determined to obey the will of God. That is exactly what I did the first few days I was home. I did something I've since come to think of as an oxymoron: I grimly obeyed the will of God. Then one evening in a prayer meeting, the Lord spoke to me.

He said, "Ben, I don't need this. If you can't obey me with anything more than grim determination, you'll just make yourself and everyone else miserable as you *bravely* (italics for sarcasm) do the will of God. If you can't serve me with joy, forget it. Go get a real job somewhere."

There can be no such thing as *grim* obedience with God. It was then I realized that joy was a choice. It's a choice

---

[6]Frederick Buechner, *The Sacred Journey* (San Francisco: Harper & Row, 1982), 85.

that comes when we choose to give thanks *in all things*. There is even a linguistic illustration of how this works spiritually. In the Greek language, the words for grace, gratitude, and joy; *charis, eucharistia*, and *chara*, respectively, all have the same root, *char*. It's a word that has to do with health and well-being. Here's how it works spiritually: grace, *charis*, naturally produces gratitude, *eucharistia*. Theologian Karl Barth says the two belong together like heaven and earth, that grace evokes gratitude like the voice of an echo, that gratitude follows grace like thunder lightning.

What then is joy? It is the subjective experience of gratitude and grace! All three are organically connected like the parts of a delicious fruit of the Holy Spirit.

That's why Paul says we can—no, he commands that we *must*—"be joyful always; pray continually; give thanks in all circumstances, for this is God's will for you in Christ Jesus" (1 Thess. 5:16–18). The pray-and-give-thanks part I understood long before the joy part. I could see how we could be commanded to pray and give thanks. But to be joyful? I had for most of my life adopted a passive stance toward joy.

Since it was a *gift* of the Holy Spirit, I said, in effect, "Anytime you're ready, Lord, lay it on me." Then I waited for something magical to happen. Nothing did.

But that night I came to understand that while I couldn't generate joy, I could choose it by choosing to obey God's command to pray continually and give thanks in all circumstances. Someone has called that "thank therapy." I can testify to its power. The vision of God is thus made sharp and clear, his mirth begins to roar in our veins, and God is glorified as we come fully alive.

You are wonderful

Like grace, gratitude, and joy, thanks and praise are organically related to each other, closely connected but separate. In thanksgiving we list God's benefits, in praise *he* is the benefit. Thanksgiving is like a child opening a gift from a parent, a new doll or a baseball mitt, and throwing her arms around her mom and dad and saying, "Thank you, thank you! It's just what I wanted. It's wonderful!" Praise is what happens when that child can pause and look up from the gift into her folks' eyes and say, "*You* are wonderful." There is, I think, in prayer and worship, a kind of ascendancy that moves from thanks to praise to wonder to awe and silence—and then back again to thanks to praise to wonder to awe to silence. Praise seems to be the singular activity of heaven. Like thanks, praise is God's due, a "species of justice." But it also does great things for us.

Praise is itself a fertile source of joy.

When our church in Irvine moved into its first building in 1982, it was a joyful occasion. We had been meeting in a school for seven years. It happened that Ken Medema, the gifted singer-songwriter-musician, was in the area, so we invited him to give a celebratory concert in our new meeting place. It was a spectacular performance, and we were grateful for what he had given us. When he finished, we rose to our feet in thunderous applause.

Later, as I reflected on the experience, it occurred to me that two things had happened: one was that in that standing ovation we had moved in our appreciation beyond his piano virtuosity to Medema himself. What he gave on the piano was spectacular. But so was he! It was more than thanks we were giving, it was praise. We had gone beyond what he had done to he himself. The second was that the praise not only let the joy inside us out, it actually fulfilled it and created yet more joy in the expression. Praising Medema together gave us more joy. To choose not to give praise, or to somehow be ordered to keep silent, would have been to abort the joy. It would have hurt.

When Jesus entered Jerusalem in triumphal procession, the crowds went wild with praise and joy. They were doing more than they knew. Jesus' religious opponents urged him to tell the crowd to keep silent. When he answered, "If they don't praise me, the stones will," he was saying there is a joy so great that it will not be squelched. Even inanimate creation would not be able to sit still in the presence of the Glorious One.

How can we?

Tuning our instruments

Praise also enlarges us. It is an exercise in our glorification. Augustine asks the question that should be in the heart of any who would call upon God:

> How shall I call upon my God, my God and my Lord, since in truth when I call upon him I call him into myself? Is there any place within me where my God can dwell? How can God come into me, God who made heaven and earth? O Lord my God, is there any place in me that can contain you?[7]

Is there any place in us that can contain God? Of course, the answer is no. Something new, something radical, must happen to us for that to happen. We must somehow be expanded.

I have a large yellow Labrador retriever named Sonja. She's everything I like about dogs: exuberantly earnest

---

[7]Augustine, *The Confessions* (Chicago: Encyclopedia Britannica, Inc., 1952), 1.

about all she does, always glad to see me, even if I've been gone for only five minutes, and tirelessly forgiving of my faults. As sweet as she is, she's but a dog—her world is a world of sounds and smells, especially smells. Her favorite organ is her nose. So if I were to try to read her one of Shakespeare's sonnets, her first response would be to sniff the book to see whether it was edible and then lose all interest in it. But what would it mean if, as I read Shakespeare, she sat up, perked up her ears, and barked her approval? It could mean but one thing: something miraculous had happened in her central nervous system, and she had been marvelously expanded in her capacity to appreciate the good, the true, and the right.

Would Shakespeare be any better because my dog liked him? No. But would she be any better? Yes!

Seeing is becoming. "The glory of God is man fully alive, and the life of man is *the vision of God*."[8] When we praise God, we adjust our vision to gaze upon the One who transforms and expands us in the gazing. "We know that when he appears, we shall be like him, for we shall see him as he is" (1 John 3:2). In praise, we anticipate Christ's appearing, and by faith, see him as he is. But we are, nevertheless, participating now in what will be. C. S. Lewis borrows an image from John Donne, describing praise as "tuning our instruments":

> The tuning of the orchestra can be itself delightful, but only to those who can, in some measure, however little, anticipate the symphony . . . even our most sacred rites, as they occur in human experience, are, like tuning, promise, not performance. Hence, like the tuning, they have in them much duty and little delight, or none. But the duty exists

---

[8]Irenaeus, Ibid., William Willimon, 64.

for the delight. When we carry out our "religious" duties we are like people digging channels in a waterless land, in order that, when at last the water comes, it may find them ready. I mean, for the most part. There are happy moments, even now, when a trickle creeps along the dry beds; and happy souls to whom this happens often.[9]

When poet George Herbert was thinking of the life-giving, soul-expanding power of praise, he described prayer as "God's breath in man, returning to his birth, the soul in paraphrase . . . the soul's blood."[10] The very breath of God that gave us life comes back into us as we breathe it out in praise. Genuine praise is God's mirth roaring in our veins—and *lungs* expanding and enlivening us.

"Acting as though . . ."

Praise is a great impetus to faith. There is a profoundly important reason for this: unbelief is first a failure at adoration. In his analysis of the human condition, Paul probes into the heart of our darkness and finds this at its root: "For although they knew God, they neither glorified him as God nor gave thanks to him, but their thinking became futile and their foolish hearts were darkened" (Rom. 1:21). Note the order: First comes the refusal to honor and give thanks to God, then follows mental darkness and futility. The reason is not hard to understand. We see what we look for; we see most clearly what we most dearly adore.

Two men were pushing their way through the crowds in New York City's Times Square. They had to shout to

---

[9]C. S. Lewis, *Reflections on the Psalms* (New York: Harcourt, Brace, Jovanovich, 1964), 97.
[10]George Herbert, "The Pulley," 183.

each other to be heard above the din. One man was a native of New York, the other was a Native American from Oklahoma.

The Native American stopped suddenly and said to his friend, "Listen! Can you hear the cricket?"

His friend thought it was a joke. "Are you kidding?" he laughed. "How could anyone hear a cricket in this bedlam? You just think you heard it."

"No, I'm not kidding," he said. "Come over here."

He walked over to a planter that was holding a large shrub and pointed at the dead leaves in the bottom. To his amazement, the New Yorker saw a cricket.

"You must have extraordinary ears," the New Yorker exclaimed.

"No better than yours," said the Native American. "It all depends on what you're listening for. Watch this."

He reached into his pocket and pulled out a handful of nickels, dimes, and quarters. Then he dropped them on the sidewalk. People from as far as two blocks away stopped and turned to see where that sound had come from.

"See what I mean?" he said. "It all depends on what you're listening for."

To listen for the right thing takes faith. Some of the best advice I ever got about how to deal with a faith crisis was something attributed to Blaise Pascal. Reportedly, he told reluctant unbelievers and others who were in some way struggling with their faith to act as though they believed, whether or not they did. Pascal believed that even something as meager as that—acting as though—would qualify as the mustard seed of faith Jesus promised would move mountains. The spirit bears a kind of internal witness to those who go only this far in faith and obedience. That advice has helped me immensely as I have time and again found myself barren in my spirit, unsure of what I believe but choosing nevertheless to praise God as though I believed. To praise God is to practice the opposite of the thing that brings unbelief in the first place.

Peek outside the cave

Praise is also an act of hope, a participation in the future, the eternal—and therefore a reality check. Plato's famous cave analogy has helped me to think about this:

Suppose a man is born in a cave and spends his entire life tied to a post, facing the wall at the rear of the cave. He cannot look to the right or the left, only forward. The light from the outside shines from behind him on the wall he faces. Occasionally people and animals walk by the cave's entrance and, as they do, their shadows are cast on the wall. These shadows and the dim light on the wall are all he ever knows of reality. To him they *are* reality. To speak of a world outside the cave, made of color and three dimensions, would be incomprehensible and unbelievable to him. But what would it mean if a mirror were held up to him, in which he could get a glimpse of the world outside the cave? Everything would change! He would then see the shadows in the context of a larger and deeper reality of depth and color.

To praise God is to gaze into a mirror and get a peek at the world outside the cave.

The cave is the "world" that St. John speaks of in his gospel and three epistles. By "world," John does not mean the creation—made by God and good, deserving our love and care. By "world," he means the evil world system of false values and pride, ruled by Satan and implacably hostile to God. Since Satan is the Father of Lies (John 8:44), his dominion is a cave of deception and falsehood, made up of "the cravings of sinful man, the lust of his eyes and the boasting of what he has and does" (1 John 2:16). The "world cave" is illusory and fading, but it exerts enormous power over our hearts and minds. According to the New Testament, it is a bitter and formidable rival of God. To be redeemed by Christ is to live no longer in darkness, but to be given the "light of life" (John 8:12). It is to begin to see things as they really are. In the praise of God we begin to see ourselves with the tens of thousands of angels in heaven, where God is visibly supreme, throughout eternity, worshiping him "who was, and is, and is to come" (Rev. 4:8).

Earthly good

To praise God is to hope in the world to come and is therefore the most practical act in this world. Occasionally I hear something like this said after a great service of worship: "That was wonderful! Too bad we have to go back to the 'real world' now."

The assumption seems to be that what happened in worship was a pleasant and therapeutic diversion, and that the real thing is out there in the rough and tumble of the world. It's the other way around! What was seen and felt in worship is the real thing. The secret is to remember what we saw and felt when we go back into the world of deception and lies.

G. K. Chesterton said the unbeliever is like a man born upside down, standing on his head, his feet "dancing upward in idle ecstasies, while his brain is in the abyss."[11] Christianity sets a man right side up. His head is placed in heaven, where it belongs, and his feet on the earth, where they belong. Now he can walk the earth and see where he

---

[11]G. K. Chesterton, *Orthodoxy* (San Francisco: Ignatius Press, 1986), 365.

is going. The saying "too heavenly minded to be any earthly good" is false. The only way to be any earthly good is to be heavenly minded! In prayer, all our work is put into a different mode, heaven in the ordinary.

Praise is also the ground of obedience. Dante paints a compelling picture of this in *The Divine Comedy*. At the very end, when he has passed through the levels of Hell and Purgatory, ascending through Heaven until he finally stands looking into the Godhead, he describes the effect gazing into the face of God has on him. Words leave him, for no mere human language can describe such a sight. But as speech departs, something remarkable is added to his desire and will: "But now my desire and will were revolved, like a wheel which is moved evenly, by the love that moves the sun and other stars."[12] The impact of looking at the unfiltered glory of God is to have his desires, his affections, his will transformed and moved by the same powerful love that makes stars and constellations, quasars and nebulae move together through this vast universe in complete harmony.

Think of your struggles with sin and temptation, of your weak will and halfhearted desire. What if these could be empowered by Dante's vision of the immeasurable glory and worth of God? They can! I return to the words of the apostle Paul: "And we, who with unveiled faces all reflect the Lord's glory, are being transformed into his likeness with ever-increasing glory, which comes from the Lord, who is the Spirit" (2 Cor. 3:18).

What Paul and Dante were describing is the promise made through the prophets of God's new covenant with humankind, and fulfilled in Jesus Christ: "I will give you a

---

[12]Dante, *The Divine Comedy*, Canto 33, The Great Books (Chicago: Houghton Mifflin Company, 1952), 157.

new heart and put a new spirit in you; I will remove from you your heart of stone and give you a heart of flesh. And I will put my Spirit in you and move you to follow my decrees and be careful to keep my laws" (Ezek. 36:26–27).

Obedience follows praise. We follow most nearly what we most dearly love:

> May I know you more clearly,
> Love you more dearly,
> And follow you more nearly
> Day by day.[13]

Am I worthy?

Helen Roseveare is a short, no-nonsense Irish doctor, with steely blue eyes and a wry wit. When I met her in 1994, she was a spry seventy and reminded me of a favorite elderly aunt or a grandmother. Just looking at her, one would not guess that she had spent the better part of her life serving Christ as a medical missionary in Zaire—or that she had been beaten and raped repeatedly by rebels during the Simba Rebellion of the early '60s. Despite her incredible suffering and subsequent emotional breakdown, she managed to come back to her work and accomplish amazing things for Christ in the jungles of that land.

I was in Kenya interviewing her for a radio program. As she spoke of her horrible experience with the rebels, a thunderstorm passed overhead and rain pounded on the tin roof of the cottage. When she was finished, she said, "I'll have nightmares tonight from this."

I said, "I would never have asked you for an interview if I had known it would have this effect on you."

---

[13]St. Richard of Chichester. Used in various musical productions.

She dismissed my remark with a short wave of her hand: "No, no. The Lord told me that if I'm going to tell this story, I can't be like a phonograph record. I'll have to feel it each time I tell it."

Then she said something incredible: "People would ask me, 'Was it worth all the suffering—what you accomplished there?' And I'd tell them, no, it's been too costly. All I got done doesn't offset what I paid for personally.

"But then the Lord spoke to me. He said, 'Helen, that's the wrong question. The question is not, *Was it worth it?* The question is, *Am I worthy?*' And I said, '*Of course you are, Lord. You are worthy.*'"

I was talking that day with a woman set right side up, her head in heaven and her feet planted firmly on the earth. Remarkable things happen to our heads and feet and hands when that happens. Because of what we have seen of heaven, we go places and do things we would never have dreamed of.

Chesterton wondered if tragedy was not something we are permitted on this earth as a kind of "merciful comedy." Why? Maybe it was because the joy and glory of heaven is too much for us now, that unmediated by the pain and struggle of this life, "the frantic energy of driving things would knock us down like a drunken farce," and we would be consumed by the "tremendous levities of the angels."[14]

Perhaps. But this much is sure: with our heads in heaven, and something of the infinite worth of God in our eyes, his praise on our lips, we are empowered and made new. God's mirth roars in our veins, a loving abandon grips

---

[14]Ibid., G. K. Chesterton, 365.

us, and we find ourselves compelled by the vision expressed by Augustine: "Lord, hast thou declared that no man shall see Thy face and live?—Then let me die, that I may see Thee."[15]

[15]Quoted in Peter Kreeft, *Three Philosophies of Life* (San Francisco: Ignatius Press, 1989), 95.

7

LONG OBEDIENCE

GEORGE MULLER, the great Victorian Christian and social reformer, tells a story of persistent prayer in his diary:

> In November 1844, I began to pray for the conversion of five individuals. I prayed every day without a single intermission, whether sick or in health, on the land, on the sea, and whatever the pressure of my engagements might be. Eighteen months elapsed before the first of the five was converted. I thanked God and prayed on for the others. Five years elapsed, and then the second was converted. I thanked God for the second, and prayed on for the other three. Day by day, I continued to pray for them, and six years passed before the third was converted. I thanked God for the three, and went on praying for the other two. These two remained unconverted.[1]

---

[1] Basil Miller, *George Muller, Man of Faith and Miracles* (Minneapolis: Bethany House Publishers, 1983), 145.

Thirty-six years later he wrote that the other two, sons of one of Muller's friends, were still not converted. He wrote, "But I hope in God, I pray on, and look for the answer. They are not converted yet, *but they will be.*"[2] In 1897, fifty-two years after he began to pray daily, without interruption, for these two men, they were finally converted—but *after* he died! Muller understood what Luke meant when he introduced a parable Jesus told about prayer, saying, "Then Jesus told his disciples a parable to show them that they should always pray and not give up" (Luke 18:1).

It's surprising to discover, given the importance Jesus attached to prayer, how little he actually said about how to pray. He gives no techniques, no methods to prayer, only a brief summary of what to pray about, the Lord's Prayer, and an urging for us to doggedly keep at it, to hang in with it, to persist and insist in prayer. In Luke 18, he encourages us to copy a widow who badgers a corrupt judge into giving her justice. In Luke 11, the chapter containing the Lord's Prayer, he tells another story of importunity, this time of a man banging away at his neighbor's door in the middle of the night until the sleepy fellow gets up and gives him food. Then Jesus says of prayer, " 'Ask and it will be given to you; seek and you will find; knock and the door will be opened to you. For everyone who asks receives; he who seeks finds; and to him who knocks, the door will be opened' " (Luke 11:9–10).

The sense of the Greek in each instance is to keep on keeping on; to repeatedly ask, seek, and knock.

Why persist?

Most of us, however, are not like Muller or the widow. Products of a culture of instant gratification, we give up if

---

[2]Ibid., 146.

we don't see a fairly quick response to our prayers. But praying, like so many matters of the kingdom of God, is like farming. Imagine a farmer turning the soil, adding fertilizer, planting seeds, sprinkling a little water—then standing over the spot for a few hours, waiting for something to happen, and when no shoot comes up, walking away, shaking his head and saying, "Well, I guess that didn't work." Farmers know better. Crops take persistent cultivation and time to yield a harvest. Like good farming, good praying demands of us a quality of character Friedrich Nietzsche called "a long obedience in the same direction."

In the two parables on prayer I just alluded to, Jesus gives a very good reason why it is worth our while to persist in prayer. Remember how parables work—the Greek word is *parabola*, which means "to lay alongside." Parables are stories, usually with one point, made either by comparison or contrast. In other words, Jesus explains a spiritual reality by taking a story from everyday life, laying it beside that truth, and then saying, in effect, "It's like this," or "it's not like this at all." In both parables on prayer, Jesus uses contrast. In the story of the widow and the callous judge (Luke 18:1–8), Jesus is saying that even someone as bad as this judge can be pressured into doing the right thing. God isn't a bit like that judge, so *how much more* can we expect him to answer our persistent prayers? It's the same in the story of the man hammering away on his neighbor's door in the middle of the night (Luke 11:5–8). God isn't a bit like the sleepy neighbor who doesn't want to get up to help his neighbor. So, *how much more* can we expect him to answer us when we come to him repeatedly with our requests?

We have a very good reason to persist in prayer.

My friend Pete Nelson is the best salesman I know. He

simply will not be turned away. Once he called on a potential client who wanted nothing to do with him. The man cursed when he saw Pete walk in the door, and shouted, "Get out of here, you (multiple expletives deleted), and don't let me ever see you walk through that front door again!" Pete went outside and analyzed what the man had said. He had said to never walk in the *front* door again. So my enterprising friend went around to the back of the business and walked in the back door. When the man saw him walk in, he exploded.

"Can't you hear? I told you to get the (expletive deleted) out of here and never to come back again."

"No, you didn't," Pete answered. "You said never to come in the front door again. I came in the back door."

The man started to rebut, but he couldn't help himself. He started to laugh, and then invited Pete into his office. Pete closed the deal soon afterward.

God is not like the client! He is not like that judge! He's like a father—or rather, a good father is something like God.

"Which of you fathers, if your son asks for a fish, will give him a snake instead? Or if he asks for an egg, will give him a scorpion? If you then, though you are evil, know how to give good gifts to your children, *how much more* will your Father in heaven give the Holy Spirit to those who ask him!" (Luke 11:11–13, italics mine).

God is like a good father. Or like a good friend. Dr. Leslie Weatherhead liked to tell the story of an old Scot who was quite ill and near death. His pastor came to call on him one morning. When he entered the bedroom and sat down beside him, he noticed another chair opposite him, placed next to the other side of the bed.

The pastor remarked, "Well, Donald, I see I'm not your first visitor today."

The old man looked puzzled and then smiled and said, "Oh, the chair. Years ago, I was having difficulty praying. I asked a friend for advice, and he suggested that I set a chair across from me when I pray, imagine God sitting in it, and talk to him as I would a good friend. It worked so well, that I've been doing it ever since."

Later that afternoon, the pastor received a call from the man's daughter. She was weeping. Between sobs she told him that her father had just died. The pastor went immediately back to the old man's house. As he spoke with the daughter, she expressed her surprise that he had died so suddenly.

"He seemed to be doing so well, I decided to take a nap," she said. "When I came back in the room he was gone. There is something I don't understand: his hand was resting on that empty chair beside his bed. Isn't that strange?"

The pastor said, "No, it's not so strange. I understand."

We have every reason to keep coming back, again and again, our whole lives, to pray to a God like that. However long he takes to answer, we know he cares, so much so that our prayers may influence what he does. That is the fundamental premise of Christian prayer, the chief reason Jesus assures us that it is worth our while to persist in it. That raises a question. Which is crazier: a widow pestering a callous judge for justice (a man who Jesus says has no fear of God or regard for man) or Christians, who have been given every assurance that God cares deeply for them and the world, but who do not pester him for the very things he has promised to those who persist?

Infinite opportunist

For many, the notion of prayer as something that can actually affect the will of God is sheer nonsense. They

reason: God knows all and is in control of all. He's infi-
nitely smarter than the brightest human being. It is therefore foolish for mere mortals to think that our desires
could have any bearing on what he will do. Rousseau
thought this way:

> I bless God for his gifts, but I do not pray to
> him. Why should I ask him to change for me the
> course of things, to work miracles on my behalf? I
> who ought to love above all the order established
> by his wisdom and maintained by his providence.[3]

In a similar vein, Immanuel Kant scorned the biblical
view of prayer as primitive mythology, calling it a "super-
stitious illusion . . . for it is no more than a *stated wish* di-
rected to a Being who needs no such information regarding
the inner disposition of the wisher; therefore nothing is
accomplished by it, and it discharges none of the duties to
which, as commands of God we are obligated; hence God
is not really served."[4]

The god they speak of is not the living God of the Bible,
the God Jesus said to come to repeatedly and importu-
nately with our requests. The Bible is clear there is nothing
we can do to change his *ultimate* will for our lives and for
the world. The final outcome of history, that God's name
be hallowed and his kingdom come and will be done are
fait accompli, fixed and sure, right now. But how God may
choose to go about achieving his goals for us and others is
open to change. His means are flexible. When it comes to
the steps in the process he may use us to bring about his
purpose. Theologian P. T. Forsyth called God an "infinite

---

[3]Quoted in Donald Bloesch, *The Struggle of Prayer* (San Francisco: Harper & Row,
1980), 73.
[4]Ibid., 73.

opportunist." In prayer, God invites us to enter into partnership with him in the working out of his immutable will in our lives and the lives of others, giving us what Pascal called the "dignity of causality."

In the mystery of the interaction between divine sovereignty and human freedom, there are some things God won't do until we ask.

Holy resistance

The mystery goes deeper. P. T. Forsyth says that not only may persistent prayer change what God will do; it may, in a sense, take the form of actually resisting what his will is in a particular instance. To resist his will can actually be to do his will. What this means is that in prayer we may sometimes resist what God wills only to be temporary and intermediary—and therefore to be transcended.

For example, I was born into a poor and relatively uneducated family. No one, on either side of my family, had ever gone to college. There were no books in my home when I was a child. That, I believe, was God's will for me. But was it also his will that I passively accept that as my fate, my foreordained situation in life? Or was it his will that I resist that circumstance and find a way to go to college, to find books and delight in them? I think it was. His lower, initial will was to be resisted in favor of his higher, more ultimate will.

At any given moment in our lives, it may be God's will that we face great pain and disappointment and loss. But it may also be his will that we resist his will in that moment, in favor of his higher and greater will. Sometimes we may beg and beg and hear him refuse, as he did Paul, and say, "My grace is enough. It's all you need" (2 Cor. 12:9, paraphrase). But other times we may come away as did the

111

blind man Bartimaeus, who would not take no for an answer, and finally got yes from Jesus (cf. Mark 10:46–52). Or it may be for us as it was with a Gentile woman from Syro-Phoenicia. She came to seek her daughter's deliverance from a demon. What she initially got from Jesus was a stiff retort. Using a figure that Jews commonly used of Gentiles, an insult, he called both her and her people "dogs": "First let the children eat all they want . . . for it is not right to take the children's bread and toss it to their dogs."

That may have turned me away, but not her. She jumped right into the fray and jabbed back, saying, "Yes, Lord . . . but even the dogs under the table eat the children's crumbs." Jesus loved it! He answered, "For such a reply, you may go; the demon has left your daughter" (Mark 7:24–30).

We may obey God as much when we push our case and plead our cause as we do when we accept his decision and say, "Yet not what I will, but what you will." But don't forget, Jesus said those words to his father *after* he had fallen to the ground and begged that it be otherwise, not before (Mark 14:32–46). How much have we missed in our lives simply because we were too frightened or too lazy or too theologically fastidious to press our case?

There's a moving scene in the television adaptation of the drama *The Miracle Worker*. It's the story of two remarkable women: a deaf and blind girl named Helen Keller, and Annie Sullivan, the person determined to teach Helen to be a human being. Helen's brother James is trying to get Annie to give up on Helen as all the others have. But Annie won't hear of it. She remembers too vividly the way her brother Jimmie had given up and died in a mental hospital. James presses her: "You don't let go of things easily, do you?"

Annie: "No. That's the original sin."

James: "What?"

Annie: "Giving up. Jimmie gave up."

James: "Perhaps Helen will teach you."

Annie: "What?"

James: "That there is such a thing as defeat. And no hope."

(Annie's face sets.)

James: "And giving up. Sooner or later, we do. Then maybe you'll have some pity on—all the Jimmies. And Helen, for being what she is. And even yourself."

(Annie sits for a moment, and then gets up silently and turns and walks away from James. She paces for a few minutes in the semi-dark room and then walks over to the bed where Helen is sleeping. She drops to her knees at the bedside. The camera takes us up to their two faces: the sleeping child and the determined teacher.)

Annie: "No, I won't let you be. No pity, I won't have it. On either of us. If God didn't mean you to have eyes, I do. We're dead a long time. The world is not something to be missed: I know. And I won't let you be till I show you it. Till I put it in your head."[5]

The trouble with our prayer lives is that we cling to God only in our weakness, when he would have us cling to him also with our strength. We're like Abraham who, planting himself in the Lord's path down to Sodom, said, "Far be it from you to do such a thing—to kill the righteous with the wicked, treating the righteous and the wicked alike. Far be it from you!" And then in language that points to Jesus' parable on prayer in Luke 18, he says, "Will not the *Judge* of all the earth do right?" (Gen. 18:25, italics mine). Holy impertinence! When's the last time you said something like that to God? Or have you ever prayed in the way Moses

---

[5]Source unknown.

told Israel to love God? "Hear, O Israel: The Lord our God, the Lord is one. Love the Lord your God with all your heart and with all your soul and with all your *strength*" (Deut. 6:4-5, italics mine).

We tend to want our prayers to be therapeutic, to leave us relaxed. More often than we wish, God would have them leave us stirred up. No wonder we get bored with prayer! No wonder we experience prayer in the same way director Billy Wilder said he experienced a film once. "The film started at 8 P.M. I looked at my watch at midnight and it was only 8:15."[6] What would happen to us if we really believed that we may affect the way God does his work, and that with holy impertinence we may actually resist him—with his blessing?

Perhaps you have seen the famous picture of the praying hands by the German painter and wood engraver Albrecht Dürer. The two hands are lifted before God with their palms together. When the great Scottish preacher and theologian P. T. Forsyth first saw a photograph of the woodcut hanging in the home of a friend, he said he wished he could have attached to it a line from John Milton that described prayer as "the great two-handed engine at our door." In Milton's time, an engine was an instrument or machine of war, used in a siege to bring down walls. Prayer, the great two-handed engine—not hands folded in resignation or passivity, but hands folded that work may be done and mountains moved.

This form of persistence spills naturally into the whole concept of actually wrestling with God in prayer, which we will discuss further in the next chapter. It is always worth our while to persist in prayer, because of who God is—not an unjust judge or a sleepy neighbor, but our Father. He

---

[6]Quoted in *Parables, Etc.* (Saratoga, Calif.: Saratoga Press, Nov. 1982), 7.

works on us by his grace, drawing us into prayer, and then allows us to work on him through our faith. It's a marvelous arrangement.

Relationship, reputation, promises

What things may we persist for in prayer? Moses' prayer after the golden calf debacle in Exodus 32 provides some exciting clues. God was very, very upset with Israel. After he had led them out of Egypt into freedom, they were trying out another god, in the form of a golden calf or bull. And now God wanted to destroy them. What followed was astounding. Moses persisted in prayer on their behalf, God relented, and Moses went on to gain quite a reputation as a man of prayer. Later, on more than one occasion, it would be only his prayers that saved the people from well-deserved extinction—he even told the Lord to destroy him, too, if he was going to destroy Israel.

For this, Moses is spoken of in Scripture as a man with whom God could speak face to face, as with a friend. Moses, the great man of prayer, persisted in prayer over three things: God's self-chosen relationship to his people, his reputation in the world, and his promises.

It's quite funny how God drew Moses into this kind of praying.

When God first told Moses of the people's sin, he said, " 'Go down, because *your people*, whom *you* brought up out of Egypt, have become corrupt.' " Note that for God it was no longer *my* people, but *Moses'* people who were sinning! Then he said, " 'Leave me alone so that my anger may burn against them and that I may destroy them.' " In other words, "Get out of my way, I'm going to wipe them out." After seeing all God did to the Egyptians when he was angry, if I were Moses I would have tripped over myself to get out of his way. But Moses didn't. He was upset with God's "redefinition" of his relationship with his people. So he said, " 'O Lord ... why should your anger burn against *your* people, whom *you* brought out of Egypt with great power and a mighty hand?' " (Ex. 32:7–11, italics mine).

Moses reminded God, "These are your people, Lord, don't wipe them out! You're the one who started the relationship; it was your idea, not ours. Don't end it now."

Next comes God's reputation. Warming to his line of argument, Moses continued, " 'Why should the Egyptians say, "It was with evil intent that he (Yahweh) brought them out, to kill them in the mountains and to wipe them off the face of the earth"?' " (Ex. 32:12). That is a vivid Hebrew way of saying, "Think of your reputation, Lord. Spare your people and be glorified. Let the nations know that you are a faithful and merciful God!"

Then come God's promises. Moses rested his case with these words: " 'Remember your servants Abraham, Isaac and Israel, to whom you swore by your own self: "I will make your descendants as numerous as the stars in the sky and I will give your descendants all this land I promised them, and it will be their inheritance forever" ' " (Ex. 32:13). In short, Moses invoked the Law of Noncontradiction and asked how God could both wipe the people out and keep his promises to the patriarchs to make of them a great nation. I like the way Luther described Moses' prayer: He flung the sack of God's promises at his feet, and he couldn't step over them!

In his name

Jesus said we can ask of God anything we want and it will be given to us—as long as it is in his name. So, think of God's self-chosen relationship to us. Think of God's glory. Think of God's promises. Then ask anything! Within those parameters is a universe of desires and delights that we may bring to God in prayer—and persist over. By them our own desires and delights are purified and refined.

Jesus was telling his disciples to pray this way when he said, "When you pray, say this: Our Father..." It's all contained in that simple opening and in the phrases that follow—our relationship to him as Father, with all the promises that go with it, and an earnest desire for his glory. When we pray, we speak to one who is our Father, whose name is to be reverenced and whose kingdom we are to desire. The Heidelberg Catechism asks, "Why hath Christ commanded us to address God thus, 'Our Father'?" [7] Its answer is, "That immediately, in the very beginning of our prayer, he might excite in us a childlike reverence for, and confidence in, God, which are the foundation of our prayer...." This is also the very foundation of persistent prayer.

Like Moses, we should persist in prayer within the context of these things. That is the way of the Psalms. Read them and note how brief the petitions are, but how extensive their meditations on God's love and majesty are. They are model prayers: state briefly your desires, but dwell on who God is. Consciously connect what you are asking with his character, for "Prayer is not overcoming God's reluctance," writes Archbishop Trench, "it is laying hold of his highest willingness."[8]

The first song I learned in church was "Jesus loves me, this I know, for the Bible tells me so; Little ones to him belong, they are weak, but He is strong." In 1949, when

---

[7] Heidelberg Catechism, Question 120, 626.
[8] Ibid., Donald Bloesch, 73.

Mao Tse Tung declared the establishment of the People's Republic of China, the country was closed to missionaries, and all Western Christians were forced to leave the mainland. The church has had a very difficult time since. For years little was known about how it was doing. What news did leak out had to be discreet. One message did get out in 1972. It was brief, and to the Chinese authorities, innocuous. It said, "The *This I Know People* are well." A vivid and powerful word to Christians, worldwide. That was who they were—the people loved by Jesus—and that has been how and why they have persisted in prayer over years of suppression and persecution.

Better than the request

What happens when we persist in prayer within this context? In the long term, we will see God's good and perfect will done. Or we may see our prayers answered better than we prayed them. We pray for silver, Luther wrote, but God often gives us gold. Other wonderful things happen, too. Our prayers get kicked up a notch. We are expanded as we ask repeatedly in Christ's name. In so doing we begin to see things more clearly, as we learn to see things through his eyes. Prayer then becomes what Emerson called "the contemplation of life from the highest point of view."[9]

Persistent prayer over a long time can leave us feeling tired and helpless. That's good! It can force us to confront our weakness and rely more on God's strength.

Three ministers were discussing the relative values of the various postures of prayer as a telephone repairman worked on the telephone system. One pastor insisted that the folding of the hands was the key to good prayer.

---

[9]Source unknown.

Another maintained that praying on one's knees was the essential. The third recommended praying flat on one's face as the most powerful prayer posture. The repairman couldn't resist: "I have found the most powerful prayer I ever prayed was upside down, hanging by my heels from a power pole, forty feet above the ground."

Most important, when we pray persistently we get to be with God. What happens to us while we pray is at least as important as the thing we pray for. The praying is often better than the thing asked. I think that is the answer to the question that was often in my mind as a young man: *Why does God wait so long to answer my prayers?* Wouldn't it be more efficient, even a greater sign of his love, to answer immediately? I've come to see that it is precisely his love that makes me wait and keep coming to him. He is more precious than anything I desire.

Aeronautics of persistent prayer

But it is hard to keep up this long obedience in the same direction. That's why it is essential to hold on to the big picture, to keep the farmer's perspective that the kingdom of God is a matter of sowing and reaping, and that between the two there is a wait.

In 1988 another pastor and I began to meet weekly to pray for revival in our churches and in the wider community of Irvine, California. We also agreed to hold monthly prayer meetings in our individual congregations to pray for the same thing. We started with a keen sense of anticipation. The church meetings were packed, and our individual meetings were stimulating. Even though he and I continued to experience a sense of God's pleasure in our times together, soon attendance at the church meetings dwindled dramatically. After a year we both were called to other churches! We've often laughed that when we prayed for revival in our churches, God chose to move us out.

Maybe there's something to that.

But what was clear as we prayed was that the people weren't embracing the vision for spiritual awakening that we felt so keenly God had put in our hearts. The next four years spent in New Providence, New Jersey, saw a similar scenario develop.

I've been dean of the chapel at Hope College for five years now, and what we have seen is the very thing I prayed would happen in Irvine and in New Providence, but which has not happened there—yet. These past five years I've discovered there have been scores, even hundreds of people, who have prayed for a spiritual awakening for Hope College for decades. My staff and I are reaping where others have sown. I still pray for Irvine and New Providence, as do their current pastors and many others. I believe someone will one day reap in these places a spiritual harvest where others have sown.

Keeping a journal has helped me to persist. Keeping a record of God's past faithfulness gives me the means to read about what I may have forgotten in the doldrums of waiting. I pray daily for my children. They're great kids, and I couldn't be more blessed or pleased with who they are. But I want it all for them; I want them to be "filled to the measure of all the fullness of God" (Eph. 3:19). Sometimes I see results, most of the time I don't.

One morning I was praying for my son, Dan, and I felt the Spirit nudge me to do two things: "Ask him what he would like prayer for. And pray that he would become a man of prayer."

A week later Dan came home from college—to wash clothes and eat, as usual—and we were talking in the kitchen. *Okay*, I thought, *now ask him what he would like prayer for.*

I asked, and he answered, "You can pray that I will pray more."

I'm glad I wrote that down in my journal, for not only can I share it with readers, but I am encouraged to keep praying and not give up. That's how Jesus said to pray—not give up. So often I feel like giving up. There's only one thing I can do when I feel that way: pray that I won't! That is, I must pray that I won't give up praying when I feel like giving up on praying. The very thing I feel weak to do will be strengthened in the doing.

In fact, I think there is a kind of "aeronautics" to persistent prayer. Isaiah 40:31 declares, "Those who hope in the Lord will renew their strength. They will soar on wings like eagles." I've watched eagles soar in the canyons of the Rocky Mountains. It's a beautiful sight to see them perched atop a cliff, then folding their wings to their sides, throwing themselves into the canyon and plummeting toward the bottom until at just the right moment they spread their wings and are shot back into heaven, gliding on thermal drafts that come up from the canyon floor. I have a friend who was a fighter pilot who told me that eagles have sensors in their nostrils that enable them to know not only the precise moment the thermals are ready, but also in their fall the precise moment they've reached the right speed to spread their wings and be thrust upward.

There's a lesson here about persistent prayer—abandon yourself to God's promises the way an eagle falls into a canyon. My tendency is to scramble up the rocks of life's canyons and just sit there and stew. But in persistent prayer, I can completely throw myself on God's mercy and pray until God acts and I am borne aloft on his power. In the meantime, I am coming to know him better and my strength is renewed.

8

HOLY CHUTZPAH

"WHY IS IT, when we talk to God, we call it prayer, but when God talks to us, we call it schizophrenia?"

That quip by Lily Tomlin has taken on many layers of meaning for me since 1986, the year we learned our seven-year-old son Joel had Tourette's Syndrome.

We noticed it first when he started playing soccer. At practice and during games, if the action was elsewhere on the field, he would stand at his position and look directly at the sun. It was painful to his eyes, and we had warned him repeatedly that it could damage them permanently, but he couldn't seem to stop. Then came other things he didn't seem to be able to control: blinking of the eyes, facial and body tics, contortions, jerks, ritual movements, random vocalizations, barking sounds, repeated clearing of the throat; and for a while the barely suppressed urge to touch the burner on the stove when it was hot.

What have I done?

Having no name for what we were witnessing, we were scared and perplexed. As I watched Joel struggle, I struggled with guilt. I wondered: *Is it something I've done to him?* Of all our kids, Joel was the one I had most often lost my temper with. Like his dad, he could be maddeningly bull-headed and combative. He was articulate beyond his years, and his words were often piercing and inflammatory. Words have great power in our household. I had frequently reacted to his words with words of my own. Over and over, in minute detail, I replayed mentally every confrontation we had ever had. Guilt and remorse pounded me like heavy surf.

Joel was scared, too. One night as Lauretta was tucking him into his bed, saying evening prayers, he spoke in the darkness, haltingly: "Mom, you know the things I do? . . . I know I'm not doing them. . . . I know Jesus wouldn't make me do them. . . ." The sentence trailed off before he spoke the alternative to Jesus and himself. When she told me what he said, we held each other in quiet terror and slipped to our knees in the living room to pray.

The moment I closed my eyes I saw, as in a vision, a large coiled python, its head resting on its giant body, its cold remorseless eyes staring. It seemed to me to be wrapped around my throat and my little boy's soul.

The worst came when I was away on a three-day prayer retreat at a desert monastery near Los Angeles. I telephoned home one evening and listened as Lauretta recounted an episode Joel had had that day with what we were later to learn was coprolalia, the obsessive repetition of obscenities. The obscenity in question was the f-word. Joel was a very moralistic child and was stricken as he whispered involuntarily, over and over, a word he loathed.

She had handled it marvelously. Taking him into the backyard she sat with him in a swing and said, "OK, let's say it out loud."

Joel was incredulous: "I can't say that awful word out loud."

"Well, can you quack it, like a duck?"

Joel has been blessed with an impish, zany sense of humor. Her suggestion was all he needed. So mother and child sat in the porch swing quacking the f-word—but not so loud that the neighbors or his siblings could hear. Then they mooed it like a cow. Then they clucked it like a chicken and crowed it like a rooster and whinnied it like a horse. Their laughter was tentative at first, then explosive. The obsession dissolved into hilarity. What a woman I married!

Holy display

But as we talked that night in the darkness—she alone at home with the kids, I in a phone booth in the desert— the weight of the day's fear was heavy on us. Normally nothing keeps me from sleep but the lack of opportunity. I lay awake for a long time that night, and awakened often after I finally fell asleep. The questions and accusations coiled tightly around my heart: *What have I done to my boy?*

A prayer for God's mercy could barely be formed in my mind, much less pass through my lips. I got up early the next day, dressed, and walked the stations of the cross at the monastery where I was staying. At each station, through tears, I thanked God that the blood of his Son, the blood of the atonement, had paid for all my sins, including what I may have done to my son.

I got back to my room twenty minutes before breakfast and sat down to read Scripture before I went to the dining hall. When I had left home, I had impulsively grabbed a devotional book off my library shelf and put it in my bag. I hadn't used it for more than a year. It was sitting on the table beside my bed that morning, so I picked it up and opened it to the readings for that particular day. The Scripture for the day was John 9. The first three verses read: "As he went along, he saw a man blind from birth. His disciples asked him, 'Rabbi, who sinned, this man or his parents, that he was born blind?' "

I knew that kind of question well. I had been asking it daily, with the tentative answer, "His parents." What I had not yet considered was Jesus' answer: " 'Neither this man nor his parents sinned,' said Jesus, 'but this happened so that the work of God might be displayed in his life.' "

An extraordinary coincidence? That on the day I was struggling as I was, the day's reading should be that? You'll never convince me that it was.

The tears came again, but now freely, joyfully. It was neither my sin nor his, but God, in his mysterious providence, doing a greater work. The coils disappeared; no more cold, remorseless eyes, but the face of the Father. God spoke, and everything that has followed with Joel has confirmed what he said. It wasn't about my sin, but the work of God, his glory, and our growth in holiness.

"God whispers to us in our pleasures, speaks to us in our consciences, but shouts to us in our pains: it is his megaphone to rouse a deaf world."[1] I have often wondered about those words of C. S. Lewis. Whatever else they may mean, they have come to mean this to me: that when he speaks thus, it is to rouse us to wrestle with him, to enter into a dialogue with the living God.

Throwing down the gauntlet

It's like the thing God does with Abraham when he announces what he plans to do to Sodom and Gomorrah.

---

[1]Quoted by Edythe Draper in *Draper's Book of Quotations for the Christian World* (Wheaton, Ill.: Tyndale House Publishers, 1992), No. 8257.

Knowing that Abraham had family in those cities, he throws down the gauntlet and says, in effect, "I'm going to destroy those cities and everyone in them, your nephew Lot and his family included. Now, what do you think of that, Abraham?"

Abraham lets him know what he thinks. He says, "How could you do such a thing? Shame on you, God! Will you sweep away the righteous with the wicked? . . . Far be it from you to do such a thing—to kill the righteous with the wicked, treating the righteous and the wicked alike. Far be it from you! Will not the Judge of all the earth do right?"

Abraham is perplexed and bewildered at what he hears; so he expostulates and attacks. Then he bargains:

"What if there are fifty righteous people in the city? Will you really sweep it away and not spare the place for the sake of the fifty righteous people in it?"

The Lord says, "If I find fifty good people there, I'll spare the city."

Moderating his pugnacity a bit, Abraham tries another angle: "Now that I have been so bold as to speak to the Lord, though I am nothing but dust and ashes, what if the number of the righteous is five less than fifty? Will you destroy the whole city because of *five* (emphasis mine) people?"

Of course, it wasn't because of five people that God was going to destroy the city. It was because of the whole city. Clever, Abe, but God isn't fooled. He answers, "If I find forty-five good people there, I will not destroy it."

Fighting more fairly, Abraham tests God's love and justice with more questions: How about forty? Or thirty? Or twenty? Or ten? Each time God answers no, he will not destroy the city if that many righteous people can be found in it (Gen. 18:16–33, partial paraphrase).

If Abraham's prayer is nothing else, it is candid.

Actually, it's more like chutzpah than candor. Once the dialogue begins, it can, and should, get that way. It took me a while. At first I was so devastated by what I saw in Joel, and so comforted that it wasn't my fault, that I could only whimper my gratitude. Lauretta and I adjusted. It's amazing how one can get used to what once seemed unbearable.

Then God kicked it up a notch one night.

Lauretta and I were having dinner with some members of our church. The husband was a male nurse working in a penitentiary. He was a good man whose skill as a chef almost offset his people skills. When, over dessert, we told him about our son's disorder, he gaped at us and launched into a speech, the substance of which was, "Oh no, not that! Anything but that! You don't want a son with Tourette's. That's horrible. No, it can't be that. Let's pray it isn't Tourette's." Apparently he had seen some shocking cases in the penitentiary. We gaped, too. His wife glared at her husband.

On the way home that night, the food sat heavily in my stomach as we contemplated the possibility that our son's disorder could get really nasty. I was mad. My prayers went from "What have I done?" to "What do you think you're doing?" Enough was enough. I had learned a good lesson about faith, I didn't need a Ph.D. I let God know how I felt. Of course he already knew before I spoke, so he wasn't surprised or shocked at what I said. My estimation of his abilities and sensitivities didn't seem to upset him, either. He knows I have flawed standards and a limited perspective. He doesn't sweat the small stuff.

I read somewhere that the ability of a couple to express anger can do wonders for their sex life. It seems there can be no warm fuzzies without their opposite (cold pricklies?). Both anger and tenderness are forms of passion. So with prayer. God doesn't mind our anger. He even relishes it, if it drives us to him instead of away from him. Better an outburst than a theologically correct and spiritually pallid rationale, and a dangling conversation. No wonder we can get so bored with prayer. God is bored, too. He wants to engage our hearts, not just our brains.

God can handle it

It was that way with Jeremiah. He got so exasperated with God and the terrible treatment God allowed him to suffer, that he virtually accused him of rape. "You have seduced me, Lord, and I have let myself be seduced; you have overpowered me: you were the stronger" (20:7 NEW JERU-SALEM BIBLE). Jeremiah was wrong, of course. God had done nothing of the sort. But that is how Jeremiah feels about what is happening in his life. And God gives no rebuke for him feeling the way he feels.

Ron Davis, a pitcher for the Minnesota Twins, was objecting to a newspaper story that quoted him as criticizing the team's management for trading away some of their best players. He told reporters, "All I said was that the trades were stupid and dumb, and they took that and blew it way out of proportion."[2] We can speak our mind with God and not be afraid that he will blow things out of proportion. He already knows what's inside. But we need to let it out for the dialogue to proceed.

If our faith in God cannot be bewildered and perplexed, we have domesticated him, and our faith is no longer in him, but in our religious systems. President Franklin Roosevelt was weary of the mindless small talk of White House receptions. Wondering if anyone was engaging in any real conversation, he conducted an experiment at a White

---

[2]Quoted in *Parables, Etc.*, Dec. 1982, 7.

House gathering. As he shook a hand and flashed that big smile he would say, "I murdered my grandmother this morning." With but one exception, the people would smile back and say something like, "You're doing a great job" or "How lovely." The exception was a foreign diplomat who responded quietly, "I'm sure she had it coming to her." If we are not shocked from time to time by the things God says and does, we have not been listening. How many of our prayers are like White House reception small talk? Does God feel about them as President Roosevelt did about the reception chatter?

Sweet perplexity

Ah, perplexity! Bitter, sweet perplexity. G. Campbell Morgan said, "Faith is the answer to a question; and, therefore, is out of work when there is no question to ask."[3] Questions are critical to faith. How else could it be with a finite human being coming to understand and trust an infinite God? No perplexity, no questions. No questions, no faith. So the God who cannot be pleased unless there is faith (Heb. 11:6) puts questions to us. To use C. S. Lewis's categories, sometimes he whispers them, sometimes he speaks them, and sometimes he shouts them. Through circumstances, he nudges us or draws us or jolts us into prayer. It may be that telephone call that shatters or that letter that disturbs. It may be the hurtful words spoken by a spouse or a friend. Perhaps it is the loss of a job or the failure of health. Suddenly we are faced with something that challenges our deepest securities, knocks away all of our props or violates everything we ever believed to be true about God and his ways.

---

[3]G. Campbell Morgan, *Twenty-Six Sermons* (Joplin, Mo.: College Press, 1969), 73.

When these things happen, we can be sure of this: that whatever else we do not know, we can know that God has taken the initiative with us to pray. Seen from this perspective, the book of Job is a book about prayer, among other things.

Where do the questions of faith lead us? To greater faith. Abraham's and Ben Patterson's wrestling with God take them to the place where they discover God to be better than they had ever before imagined. Of Abraham's wrestling, Morgan says, "God is not only better than our fears, he is better than our hopes, better than the very best we had dared to suppose. We stop at ten. God takes care of the one.... As Abraham's mathematics decreased from fifty to ten, his faith increased inversely."[4] Jacob wrestles and becomes Israel, a new man. When Job wrestles, though he has not one of his questions answered, he says in the end that it is more than enough, that he is satisfied and fulfilled. For while before he had only heard about God, now he has seen him. To gain even a glimpse of the glory and goodness of God is reason enough to wrestle.

It's true, you know. God's glory is enough. I'll never forget sitting in an evening service in my church and knowing this was true. It had been a tough year. I didn't like being a pastor anymore, but couldn't think of anything else I could do. The choir was performing a beautiful piece. This is hard to explain, and may sound a little weird to someone who has never had the experience, but in the beauty of the music I got a glimpse of God's transcendent beauty and goodness, just for a moment. It was like a spear of longing and delight had pierced my heart. The ache was exquisite. My first thought was, *Lord, you are enough. I'll do this lousy job forever if you let me walk with you and get just a peek at you*

---

[4]Ibid., 74.

130

once in a while. There is no pain or perplexity so heavy that it outweighs his glory. And it would seem that both are necessary for us to see it.

Holy war

So God "loves that holy war," writes P. T. Forsyth, using the image of two Greco-Roman wrestlers. "Cast yourself into his arms not to be caressed but to wrestle with him. . . . He may be too many for you, and lift you from your feet. But it will be to lift you from earth, and set you in the heavenly places which are theirs who fight the good fight and lay hold of God as their eternal life."[5]

Did my wrestling end that morning in the monastery? No. Or after I recovered from the nurse's speech? No. Has God become grander? Yes.

Joel, who is now a freshman in college, agrees. I asked him if I could write about him and our struggle. He looked at me with level gaze and said quietly, but emphatically, "Absolutely, Dad." He is growing into an extraordinary young man. He has both physical health and an intuitive sense of things spiritual that set him apart; not in spite of his struggle but because of it. I don't just love him, I admire him. I want to be like him when I grow up.

God's grace has been sufficient in countless ways. After we got a diagnosis and the word got out in the church, we found on our doorstep one morning a list of names written into time slots. It was a sign-up of church members who would pray for Joel, at fifteen-minute intervals, every Tuesday, from 6 A.M. to 11 P.M. That happened for years. For several, it continues to the present day. What it meant for Joel and his spiritual development and for the church was

---

[5]P. T. Forsyth, *The Soul of Prayer* (London: Independent Press, LTD., 1954), 92.

incalculable. This side of eternity, we will never know its significance. All the sermons I preached on prayer did not have the effect on the prayer life of the church that Joel's illness had. The pastor became the "pastored." What a concept: Wrestle with God and you will always find him to be more than you bargained for.

Joel's symptoms have been manageable ever since. Whenever I am tempted to say that he has a mild case of the syndrome, I am reminded of the fact that he has been much prayed for. I also know that Tourette's Syndrome is often unpredictable, that it can wax and wane over time and that there is no absolute "trajectory" for the disorder. It can get worse or better, or better and worse over the years. Joel knows that, too. But God's grace will also be sufficient over time. How will I know that? By continuing to wrestle with him over whatever is ahead. There's always more than you bargain for.

Last summer I spoke publicly of our struggle for the first time at a Christian conference center on the West Coast. The response was more than we bargained for. People opened their hearts to us. One dear woman had a son with a rather severe case of Tourette's. She was so shamed and embarrassed by his tics that she had never even acknowledged them to her best friend—a woman she met with in her home several times a week and who could not have been unaware that something was amiss with the child. There they were, close friends but closed off to each other. What had that meant to her relationship with God? It was a tender joy to see the fear and tension leave her face as she spoke with my wife.

Other things were set in motion by this perplexity. We know that moderate use of alcohol is probably not a realistic option for Joel, given the prevalence of obsessive-compulsive behavior among people with Tourette's. As a result of this, I began to ponder whether I should even keep alcoholic beverages in the house. It took a lot of pondering, since nobody enjoys a beer more than I do. The pondering became wrestling when I began to think about my own use of alcohol. It dawned on me that I planned my days around the beer I would have when I came home from work. Around two in the afternoon I would begin to wonder if we had any beer in the refrigerator. *Should I stop and pick up some on the way home?* And when I got home I had to admit that I really didn't want to talk to anyone until I opened a beer and had my "quiet time" with my cold little friend. I wasn't drinking to excess in terms of volume, but I was in terms of interest. Compulsive, addictive? Perhaps. In any case, I am now a teetotaler, and life has become so much simpler. All because of the wrestling with God over Joel. Again, more than I bargained for.

The best has been the laughter

The best has been the laughter. When we were first confronted with Tourette's, we never dreamed laughter would come, but it has. We have sat around the dinner table and laughed with Joel about the weird and often funny things that can happen to someone with Tourette's. The episode with the f-word was the antecedent. Like many with the disorder, Joel is extremely bright, creative, and blessed with a zany, rapid-fire Robin Williams kind of wit. He has said, only half-jokingly, that he thinks those with Tourette's are one step above, on the evolutionary ladder, those who are normal. I'm not willing to go that far. But hey, gratitude for God's grace should make us a little excessive in our judgments.

Are we crazy?

Lily Tomlin's crack about prayer and schizophrenia is

probably accurate as it applies to the way many in our culture and in the church think about such things. I admit that I have even wondered out loud, *Is that really you, God? Or just my wishful thinking?* Unlike some theological points, questions like this rarely have a neat answer. But I've come to believe that God is not nearly as fastidious in matters of faith as we may like him to be, and that when faith moves mountains, there is bound to be rubble.

Earlier in my Christian experience, I was afraid to name something as the voice of God for fear I might be wrong and look dumb. Then it occurred to me that I was probably missing a lot because of my fear of how I might look. Which was worse—to always look cool and rational but risk missing the voice of God? Or to risk looking a little credulous and crazy once in a while, but hear God, at least more often than I had been? I've opted for the latter. Call it prayer and schizophrenia if you will, but I think trying to look cool was something we were supposed to have given up in junior high. Peter Marshall observed, "It is a fact of Christian experience that life is a series of troughs and peaks. In his efforts to get permanent possession of a soul, God relies more on the troughs than on the peaks. And some of his special favorites have gone through longer and deeper troughs than anyone else."[6]

Abraham, Moses, Jeremiah, and Paul—all great and very special wrestlers—would agree. It makes me feel kind of special, too.

[6]Peter Marshall, source unknown.

9

LISTENING SERVANT

A WOMAN NAMED MARY GEEGH lives in my town. Now in her nineties, she is bedridden in a nursing home. She wrote a wonderful little book called *God Guides*, telling of her experiences of hearing God's voice during her long career as a missionary in India. I've read it many times. Her method, if one can call it that, was simple. When she needed to hear from the Lord about something—which was about every day—she would sit down with a pad and pencil, ask the Lord for his wisdom in the situation, listen quietly until he spoke, write down what she heard, and then do it.

Just like that.

If she didn't hear anything, she wouldn't do anything. Once when she was at odds with a fellow missionary and stumped over what to do to heal the breech, she listened for God's wisdom and heard the Spirit say, "Give her an egg." Perplexed, but obedient, she did what the Lord said to do, half apologizing to her colleague for what seemed to be a foolishly irrelevant act, given the tension between them. As it turned out, the gift of the egg had extraordinary significance for her alienated sister, since she needed exactly one more egg to feed her family that evening and had been wondering where she could find one. Mary's act of obedience to what some call "the inner voice" showed her sister not only that she truly desired reconciliation but that God did too, powerfully so. To read her book is to read of a woman who had this kind of thing happen over and over again.

True, it's a little odd the way she would almost routinely hear the voice of God. Or should I say, uncommon?

Most of us have not had her experience, but everyone I've known who has read of it has expressed a wistful longing to hear from God in the same simple and unaffected way. Prayer is a dialogue, a conversation with God, not a monologue or soliloquy. We need to learn to listen and hear his side of the conversation, and it should not be uncommon for us to hear him say something. He has promised in his word, "If any of you lacks wisdom, he should ask God, who gives generously to all without finding fault" (James 1:5).

One morning recently, I woke up feeling heavy and depressed about a situation at the college. There had been a great deal of controversy over a theological stance my staff and I had taken; I had received a lot of criticism and personal attack. I was having second thoughts. It's one thing to get hammered for doing the right thing, it's another thing to get hammered for doing the wrong—or the stupid—thing.

I was inquiring of the Lord: Was I doing the right thing, seeing that it would stir up so much anger? Should I have taken a softer position, a more gentle approach? Was my timing off? I opened my Bible to the daily reading, and the psalm happened to be Psalm 130, which begins, "Out of the depths I cry to you, O Lord. . . ." That matched my mood perfectly! I prayed that verse again and again with deep feeling, grateful to God for the voice his Word gave to my emotions. Since the psalm is a penitential psalm, I wondered if God were indeed telling me that I should back off the position I had taken.

But as I prayed, my eyes wandered to the center of the page to a column of cross-references parallel to that verse. They related to the psalm I had read several days before, Psalm 129—yes, I had missed a few days of Bible reading.

It's a psalm that begins with "They have greatly oppressed me from my youth ... but they have not gained the victory over me." Certainly a psalm of a different stripe, a psalm not of penitence but of resistance! It prays, in effect, "Lord, they have treated me terribly, but they haven't gotten the better of me." Years before, on another occasion of reading that psalm, I had highlighted the cross-references for those words. They were the cross-references my eyes fell upon that morning, the words that God spoke to Jeremiah: " 'Get yourself ready! Stand up and say to them whatever I command you. Do not be terrified by them, or I will terrify you before them. Today I have made you a fortified city, an iron pillar and a bronze wall to stand against the whole land. . . . They will fight against you but will not overcome you, for I am with you and will rescue you,' says the Lord" (1:17–19).

Of course, I found the content and the *timing* of these words stunning, given my situation.

But I was wondering if I had fallen into a pit of subjectivity and self-justification when I met with my wife for our morning prayer time. Had I made the Bible a kind of Rorschach inkblot upon which to project my own perceptions and desires? I shared with her what I had experienced and read, and watched her eyes grow wide as she told me the Jeremiah passage was the exact text she had been praying over that morning, line for line, as part of her daily reading. Since that morning it hasn't become any more pleasant to take the stand I have taken, but it has been easier.

Sweet voice

The promise of God to give wisdom to those who ask for it has been vividly real to me as I have cultivated an attitude of quiet listening, of being open to hearing his end of the dialogue. I spend more time alone, in silence, than I used to—rising early to be in solitude and stillness. I joke with my friends that the chief spiritual danger in getting up so early is self-righteousness, the smugness that can creep into my soul when I know that as I am praying, others are sleeping. But in all honesty, I get up not to achieve an elite level of spiritual athleticism; I get up because it is so good and pleasant to do so. I can hardly call it a discipline anymore. It is so delicious, so ineffably sweet to hear the Lord, the Good Shepherd speak, or even to hope that he might. It isn't so much that God speaks directly during those times; rather, the stillness prepares me to be alert to those whispers and nudges I might receive from him as I drive my car or walk across campus. Fernando Ortega sings a song that speaks of how desolate we are until God speaks, and how richly blessed we are when he does:

> O Thou, in whose presence
> my soul takes delight,
> On whom in affliction I call,
> My comfort by day
> and my song in the night,
> My hope, my salvation, my all!
> Where dost Thou dear Shepherd,

resort with Thy sheep,
To feed them in pastures of love?
Say why in the valley of death
should I weep?
Or alone in this wilderness roam?
O why should I wander
an alien from Thee?
Or cry in the desert for bread?
Thy foes will rejoice
when my sorrows they see,
And smile at the tears I have shed.
He looks and ten thousands
of angels rejoice,
And myriads wait for His word.
He speaks, and eternity
filled with His voice,
Reechoes the praise of the Lord.
Dear Shepherd, I hear,
and will follow Thy call,
I know the sweet sound of Thy voice.
Restore and defend me,
for Thou art my all,
And in Thee I will ever rejoice![1]

The Paraclete

Thoughts like these are preposterous to postmodern sensibilities—only the arrogantly foolish could believe that almighty God would speak to a mere fallible, contingent human. But they are in perfect accord with what biblical revelation tells us of the God to whom we pray, who calls us each by name, numbers the hairs on our head, and even

---

[1]"O Thou, in Whose Presence," sung by Fernando Ortega, *This Bright Hour,* Myrrh Records, 1997; Words: Joseph Swaim, Music: Freeman Lewis, Arrangement: Fernando Ortega and John Andrew Schreiner.

helps us to pray. The Bible says God gives us his Spirit to help us in our weakness since "we do not know what we ought to pray for, but the Spirit himself intercedes for us with groans that words cannot express. And he who searches our hearts knows the mind of the Spirit, because the Spirit intercedes for the saints in accordance with God's will" (Rom. 8:26–27).

Jesus called the Spirit the "Counselor" or "Comforter" or "Helper" or "Advocate," depending on how the word he used is translated. The variety of words indicates the difficulty of finding an English word to match the Greek word used by Jesus. The word, *parakletos*, is a compound of two words, *para*, "alongside" and *kletos*, from *kalein*, "to call." *Parakletos* was used by the Greeks to describe someone called to one's side for help and encouragement. In its verb form, that is exactly what it means: to help and to encourage. Paul, for example, tells the Colossians that he is sending them his friend Tychicus so he may encourage, be a *paraclete* to their hearts. To the Corinthians, Paul describes God as the "Father of compassion and the God of all comfort, who comforts us in all our troubles" (2 Cor. 1:3–4). *Comfort* is the word the translators of the NIV used for *paraclete*. What Jesus is saying is that just as he came alongside his disciples in their life's journey, so he will continue to come alongside them in the *paraclete*, the Holy Spirit.

Surgeon Paul Brand tells a story that provides a gripping picture of the work of the *paraclete*.

He was a junior doctor in a London hospital when one day he came into the room of an eighty-one-year-old cancer patient named Mrs. Twigg. Her cancer was in her throat and, as he describes it, this "spry, courageous woman ... had asked that we do all we could medically to prolong her life, and one of my professors removed her larynx and the malignant tissue around it."

Brand received an urgent summons to her ward one day, and walked in to find her bleeding profusely from her mouth. He guessed immediately that an artery on the back of her throat had eroded. There was only one thing he knew to do to stop the bleeding: apply pressure. They had only to wait for the surgeon and the anesthetist to arrive. Looking into her terror-stricken eyes as she fought the urge to gag, he assured her that he would not remove his finger until it was absolutely safe to do so. He describes what happened:

> We settled into position. My right arm crooked behind her head, supporting her. My left hand nearly disappeared inside her contorted mouth, allowing my index finger to apply pressure at the critical point. I knew from visits to the dentist how fatiguing and painful it must be for tiny Mrs. Twigg to stretch her mouth open wide enough to surround my entire hand. But I could see in her intense blue eyes a resolution to maintain that position for days if necessary. With her face a few inches from mine, I could sense her mortal fear. Even her breath smelled of blood. Her eyes pleaded mutely, "Don't move—don't let go!" She knew, as I did, if we relaxed our awkward posture, she would bleed to death.
>
> We sat like that for nearly two hours. Her imploring eyes never left mine. Twice during the first hour, when muscle cramps painfully seized my hand, I tried to move to see if the bleeding had stopped. It had not, and as Mrs. Twigg felt the rush of warm liquid surge up her throat she gripped my shoulder anxiously.
>
> I will never know how I lasted that second hour. My muscles cried out in agony. My fingertip grew totally numb. I thought of rock-climbers who have

held their fallen partners for hours by a single rope. In this case the cramping four-inch length of my finger, so numb I could not even feel it, was the strand restraining life from falling away.

I, a junior doctor in my twenties, and this eighty-one-year-old woman clung to each other superhumanly because we had no choice—her survival demanded it.[2]

Finally the surgeon came, and they were wheeled into the operating room. There, as everyone stood poised with gleaming tools, he slowly removed his finger as her aged hand clutched his wrist. When his finger was totally removed, a smile spread across her bruised lips. The clot had held. She would be all right. With no larynx, only her eyes could express her gratitude.

"She knew how my muscles had suffered," writes Brand. "I knew the depths of her fear. In those two hours in the slumberous hospital wing, we had become almost one person."[3]

After telling this story, Dr. Brand made two comments: In all of his years as a physician, the thing that keeps coming back to him time and again from his patients is that when they are on their backs and at the very extremes of their ability to believe and to endure, only one kind of person can help. That person rarely has any answers to their questions, he seldom has a winsome and effervescent personality. It is always someone who does not judge or give advice but who will simply be there with them in their suffering, who will be present, perhaps to share tears, or a hug, or a lump in the throat.

---

[2]Dr. Paul Brand and Philip Yancey, *Fearfully and Wonderfully Made* (Grand Rapids: Zondervan, 1980), 202.

[3]Ibid., 203.

Stated theologically, the most helpful person is a *paraclete*, one who comes alongside.

Brand's other comment came by way of a quotation by John V. Taylor about the Holy Spirit. He said, "The Holy Spirit is the force in the straining muscles of an arm, the film of sweat between pressed cheeks, the mingled wetness on the back of soft clasped hands. He is as close and as unobtrusive as that, and as irresistibly strong."[4]

That is the God of the Bible. He knit us together in our mother's womb, knows each of our words before we speak them—and he speaks. Why should we find that surprising? Such a God is not only a spiritual reality, but an emotional necessity.

Psychologist Rollo May argued in his 1960s bestseller, *Love and Will*, that our age can be best characterized by the word *apathy*, meaning "a state of feelinglessness, the despairing possibility that nothing matters." He said the opposite of love is not hate, but apathy—being uninvolved, detached, unrelated; the violence of our times, he said, is the direct result of "*affectionlessness* as an attitude toward life."[5] In an age of mass communication, the average person is anonymous and alienated. Dozens of TV personalities come smiling into his living room each evening. He knows them all, but is himself completely unknown. He can spend years in a factory, a shop, an office, a family, even a church—without meeting anyone who takes the slightest interest in him as a person, in his intimate concerns, in his difficulties, in his secret aspirations.

When one cannot touch or be touched, violence then springs up as a kind of demonic need for contact. In this bizarre state of affairs, painful for anyone to bear, the

---

[4]Ibid., 193.
[5]Rollo May, *Love and Will* (New York: Norton, 1969), 30.

mood of the unknown person becomes, "If I cannot affect or touch anybody, I can at least shock you into some feeling, force you into some passion through wounds and pain; I shall at least make sure we both feel something, and I shall force you to see me and know that I also am here."[6]

Significantly, apathy comes from the Greek words *apatheia*, without, and *pathos*, feeling—the term used by first-century Greeks to describe God. They reasoned that God could not at the same time be God and feel for people, because God, by definition, is high above us and splendidly removed from the sweat and blood of human life. To be affected by us would be to make him less than us.

That was what made the gospel so scandalous to the Greek mind. It told of a God who entered human history in Jesus Christ, feeling all we feel and suffering all we suffer. The word became flesh and "moved into the neighborhood," to use Eugene Peterson's paraphrase of John 1:14 (THE MESSAGE). That is, the God assumed in Christian prayer is personal, he knows us, he hears us, he listens, really listens, and he speaks.

In the film *Oh, God!*, George Burns portrays God as an approachable and likable person with a good sense of humor and a keen appreciation of the foibles of being a human being. When he first appears to the young man played by John Denver, he so impresses him with his miracles that the young man becomes attached to him and detached from his fellow human beings. To remedy this, God announces that he will put on no more miraculous displays and will disappear from sight. The young man is heartbroken: "But won't I be able to talk to you anymore?" he cries. God smiles. "You talk," he says, "I'll listen."

This was Hollywood's lame attempt to make sense of

---

[6]Ibid., 31.

the apparent silence of God in human affairs—to make him out as a kind of giant nondirective therapist in the sky, a cosmic Carl Rogers. God doesn't say much, but he's a good listener. But a good listener will say something. He'll do more than just nod and smile, sphinxlike. A good listener gets involved. God is a good listener. In fact, he is so involved that we would never speak to him had he not first spoken to us. God is the great initiator.

In this sense, P. T. Forsyth was right when he said all our prayers are answers to God's.

Eye opener

So God speaks. But how can we hear his voice?

By praying obediently, being willing to do what we hear if we hear it. When George MacDonald said, "Obedience is the opener of eyes," I believe he was exegeting the words of Jesus to skeptics: "If anyone *chooses* to do God's will, he will *find out* whether my teaching comes from God or whether I speak on my own" (John 7:17, italics mine). We won't know until we're willing to obey. Obedience is the basis of biblical epistemology.

I first began to understand this the summer between my ninth- and tenth-grade years.

My next-door neighbor was two years ahead of me in school and a bright and argumentative nonbeliever. Many warm evenings we would argue about the existence of God until late at night. To a stalemate. It was so clear to me that God did exist, it was obvious to him that he didn't, or so he argued.

One evening the insight came to me from the parable Jesus told about the rich man and the beggar, Lazarus. In the parable, Jesus told of how the rich man, after a life of callous selfishness, ended up burning in hell and watching from afar the bliss of Lazarus in heaven at Abraham's side. The rich man begged for help. Would Abraham please dip his finger in water to cool his tongue? No, he couldn't. Would he then send Lazarus back from the dead to warn his brothers who awaited the same fate if they did not change their ways? No, he wouldn't. Abraham replied, "They have Moses and the Prophets; let them listen to them."

The formerly rich man didn't think that was enough. But if someone actually came back from the grave to warn them—perhaps like Marley to Scrooge in Dickens' *A Christmas Carol*—then they would believe and repent, wouldn't they? Abraham's answer is instructive: "If they do not listen to Moses and the Prophets, they will not be convinced even if someone rises from the dead" (Luke 16:19–31). Even seeing won't be believing if they aren't willing to obey.

So I put the question to my friend: "If God appeared before us, right here, on the front porch of this house, and you knew beyond any doubt that it was actually God standing there, would you commit your life to him to obey all his laws?"

In a moment of unguarded candor, he said, "Well, I'd have to think about that." His answer explained his inability to believe, to know. I've come to believe that I won't hear from God unless I am first willing to act on what I've heard. God hides himself from those who refuse to obey, so that "they may be ever seeing but never perceiving, and ever hearing but never understanding; otherwise they might turn and be forgiven!" (Mark 4:12).

Listening disciplines

Asking God to speak is subject to the same rule that asking God to do anything else is.

Jesus said, "Ask whatever you wish and it will be given you." The condition for that kind of answered prayer is in the line that precedes it: "If you remain in me and my words remain in you" (John 15:7). Remaining in Jesus is the condition. The Greek word for *remaining* means literally "to dwell" or "to take up residence." This word, and what it conveys, was so important to Jesus that he used it eleven times in the first ten verses of John 15. He was saying that prayer must flow out of a relationship of fellowship and communion with him. Answered prayer comes from his living in us and our living in him. It is prayer that is patterned after the prayer life of Jesus himself. His whole life was lived in total and unbroken communion with God. There was absolutely no distinction between his will and his Father's will. He could say to the Pharisees that "the Son can do nothing by himself; he can do only what he sees his Father doing, because whatever the Father does the Son also does" (John 5:19). In another place, Jesus told the crowd gathered to hear him preach, "The one who sent me is with me; he has not left me alone, for I always do what pleases him" (John 8:29). Before he commanded the dead man Lazarus to rise from the dead, he lifted his eyes to God and prayed, " 'Father, I thank you that you have heard me. I knew that you always hear me, but I said this for the benefit of the people standing here, that they may believe that you sent me' " (John 11:41–42).

Note that it was almost as though he need not even ask God to raise Lazarus, but only to say the word, because his will was so conformed to God's will. This is prayer at its highest and deepest. It is prayer that is in communion with the risen Jesus, that lives and abides and dwells in him. "Keep close to the New Testament Christ," writes P. T. Forsyth, "and then ask for anything you desire in that contact. Ask for everything you can ask in Christ's name, i.e., everything desirable by a man who is in Christ's kingdom of God, by a man who lives for it at heart, everything in tune with the purpose and work of the kingdom in Christ."[7] In that kind of *obedient* praying, it is the most natural of events to hear the voice of the living God speak.

There are some ways, discipline if you will, to learn to pray obediently.

One way is to pray Scripture. Naturally the great prayers of Scripture, of Jesus, of the prophets and apostles, lend themselves to this. Almost any text can be meditated on and formed into a prayer. The value of praying Scripture is that it can train us to feel what it expresses, to think God's thoughts after him, and thus to tune our hearts to hear God's voice in other ways. The same can be said of some of the prayers of godly saints through the ages, such as the prayer of St. Francis: "Lord, make me an instrument of Thy peace." These represent the distilled wisdom of God's people and can train our hearts in obedient prayer. My own practice has been to pray through the Psalter each month, five psalms a day. I have also memorized all of the prayers of St. Paul, praying them over and over until they become my own. I believe this discipline has trained my heart and my ears to hear the Lord.

Another discipline is to take some minor risks in prayer—to respond to nudges of the Holy Spirit. Most of us have felt moved from time to time in prayer to make a telephone call or write a note to someone. For years I regarded those thoughts as distractions. Now I see them as possible nudges from the Lord to do something he wants done. I have often been amazed and delighted at what happens when I follow those promptings. I have often been the beneficiary of those who did.

---

[7] P. T. Forsyth, 66.

One spring day in 1993, I was so discouraged I didn't know how I could go on with my work. I prayed with my wife over my anguish and went outside for a long walk, hoping that the physical activity would renew my spirits. It didn't. I walked back into the house and heard the telephone ringing; the last thing I wanted to do was pick up the telephone. I usually screen my calls by listening to the voice on the other end of the line coming through the answering machine. The voice was that of a woman who was new to the church. She was apologizing for calling at home, but felt there was something I needed to know. Against my normal impulses, I picked up the telephone. She apologized again and said, "I hope you don't think I'm crazy, but as I was praying this morning you came to mind, along with a Bible reference I did not know. I looked it up and have no idea if it would mean anything to you, but I felt that somehow I would be disobedient to God if I didn't give it to you."

She apologized again and then gave me the passage. It was Hebrews 10:35–39. She apologized once more, said good-bye, and hung up. The passage read:

> So do not throw away your confidence; it will be richly rewarded. You need to persevere so that when you have done the will of God, you will receive what he has promised. For in just a very little while, "He who is coming will come and will not delay. But my righteous one will live by faith. And if he shrinks back, I will not be pleased with him." But we are not of those who shrink back and are destroyed, but of those who believe and are saved.

Need I say that those words were meaningful to me? I have since had them written in calligraphy and framed as a memorial to God's faithfulness to speak when I needed a word from him and to a woman's faithfulness to risk in obedience to God, to act on a nudge. Sometimes I wonder in frustration why God doesn't speak to me. Does God wonder in frustration why it is that he has spoken, and I haven't listened—because I have been too busy or rationalistic or timid to obey?

Grammar of existence

Closely allied to praying obediently is praying humbly. That means keeping clear on what philosopher Peter Kreeft calls the "grammar of existence" and remembering that God is God and we are not. God reserves the right to speak when and what and how he desires. We may place no demands on him. We may pray the prayer of Mary before and after God speaks: "I am the Lord's servant, may it be to me as you have said." Sometimes God will answer our question with another question.

A friend went to his church on a Saturday night to lead a small prayer gathering. He waited, but no one showed up. He was alone in an empty church, sitting in that peculiar sort of Saturday-night deadness churches can have, feeling the acute kind of disappointment one feels when no one shows up. At first he thought, *What a waste of time, Lord.* Then he decided to sit and be still—and he realized he was, as he described it, "listening in silence." He listened and he heard a question from God: "Will you honor me?" It was a deep and probing question, one that has stuck with him and that he is trying to apply to other areas of his life. It's much harder to hear a good question than an obvious directive. A question requires more of us—the humility to engage God on the level he chooses. He who asks the questions sets the agenda.

We should be suspicious of those telling us prayer taps

into a divine power source. The image is of a utility line, which we can switch on or off—whenever we wish. It's there when we need it and waiting to be used when we don't need it. This view of prayer, however, betrays our hubris and consumerism. It makes God a handyman we can hire out from time to time for various projects. There is power in prayer, all right, as Virginia Stem Owens writes, "It is fearsome to the last degree. It is not a power that can be harnessed. The images from the Bible shatter us with their uncontrollable force. A dove descends. Tongues of fire flame out. An angel appears. A bush burns. A mountain trembles. A whirlwind answers. God invades."[8]

Owens recounts how she decided that after she had laid out her requests before God in her evening prayers, she would then listen for God to say something back to her. She waited in the darkness for something to come, but heard nothing. Finally, tired and dissatisfied, she went to sleep. The night passed, but in the early morning hours, just before dawn, she found herself awake and weeping. There was in her mind the memory of a spinster aunt who had come to live with her family when Owens was a young adolescent. Her family had just moved, and she had been promised a room of her own in the move. But with her aunt's arrival, it was her brother who got the new room and Owens who got a roommate, a semi-invalid aunt who had been forced to live with relatives her whole life. Over the weeks and months that followed, Owens barely concealed her bitterness at this injustice, showing it in a thousand subtle and caustic ways. She had carried the grudge her whole life:

---

[8]Virginia Stem Owens, *Christianity Today*, November 19, 1976: 17–21.

But now, in this early morning light, I was feeling for the first time the scalding shame this elderly woman must have felt. Moving from house to house, never having one of her own. Totally dependent on the good graces of nieces and nephews for the very necessities of life. Never in all my years at home, or indeed until now, had I given a single thought to how she felt in the situation. But now I was getting a full dose of it—the pride that had to be swallowed daily in a galling gulp. It was more bitter than I could bear.[9]

The next evening she repeated the same exercise, offering her petitions to God and then listening awhile before drifting off to sleep. The same kind of thing happened the next morning over another incident from her past, again with the same shattering results. She wasn't quite so sure she wanted to hear from God anymore!

Such has been the experience of the Jeremiahs and Pauls and other great men and women of prayer down through the centuries. They pray for God to change things in their world, and he begins by changing them. They tell God what is on their minds and he tells them what is on his mind: them!

"Awful things happen to people who pray," says Owens. "Their plans are frequently disrupted. They end up in strange places.... The well-worn phrase, 'Prayer changes things,' often meant to comfort, is as tricky as any Greek oracle."[10]

It takes humility to listen to God, because it may be humbling to hear from him.

Constant prayer is another way to cultivate an ear to

---

[9]Ibid., 13.
[10]Ibid., 21.

hear the voice of God. Jesus said, "I am the vine; you are the branches. Apart from me you can do nothing" (John 15:5). He is the sole source of our life. Branches receive no life-giving sap unless they remain in constant contact with the vine. We receive no life unless we stay in constant contact with Christ. Thankfully, our contact with him is not dependent on our resolve to hold on to him but on his resolve to hold on to us. He wants us to live and dwell in him more than we want to live and dwell in him. But because God wills communion with us, we are therefore exhorted to have communion with him, as branches in a vine.

That was the secret of Jesus' life: his constant contact with God.

For the sake of the whole

Early in my Christian life I had impressed on me the critical importance of a daily quiet time, of time set aside to be alone with God. Over the years I have learned that lesson well. My favorite time of the day is the time I spend, usually early in the morning, alone with God. But I have begun to realize that I can treat that time like a physical workout: once I have done it, I'm done with it until the next day. I don't give God much thought the rest of the day. I was disdainful of those who told me they didn't have time to spend an hour in prayer each day, so they prayed in their car on the way to work and throughout the day as the opportunity presented itself.

I now repent of my disdain. But it's not either/or—either I pray for an hour in the morning or I pray through the day. It's both/and.

The purpose of setting apart an hour in the morning is so that all the other hours may be God's as well. Theologian Stephen Winward opened me up to this insight: We sanctify a part not so we may forget about the whole, but for the sake of the whole. We dedicate an hour to the Lord, so all our hours may be his.

Well known is that practice to the medieval monk Brother Lawrence, who "practiced the presence of God" as he went about his daily duties in the monastery. His daily duties consisted chiefly of scrubbing pots and pans in the kitchen. But as he scrubbed, he might comment to Jesus on how dirty a pan was. As he stacked the dishes high, he would thank the Lord for how well he had provided for him and his brother monks. This was not all his prayer, for there were also the high and holy moments in the quietness of his room and the sanctuary when he prayed on his knees. But that was of one piece with the low, but no less holy, moments when he scrubbed dishes and spoke with Jesus about the scrubbing.

I read about how Ronda Chervin, a housewife and associate professor of philosophy at Marymount University, has found ways to pray throughout her day. She prays while ironing, for the person whose clothing she is working on. She prays while walking down the street, for each person she meets. She prays when unable to see a friend, "wrapping my love with a prayer and sending it through the Lord."[11] She prays when thinking of her old friends, remembering their needs before God. She prays upon entering each new phase of the day or when facing a difficult situation, speaking to the Lord and thanking him that she is not alone and that he makes all things work together for the good.

Apricot pie a la mode?

Maybe the last and best thing to be said about listening for God's voice is that it can be such a joy, such *fun*, and

---

[11]Source unknown.

so funny. God really is more interested in being heard than we are to hear him. It delights him to speak to his children and for them to hear. Even in the seriousness of the matters that concern us, we can be delighted, too.

As I mentioned earlier, after fourteen years of pastoring a church in Irvine, California, I was extended a call to pastor a church in New Providence, New Jersey. To accept the church's invitation would mean going from a church that I had founded to a church that was over two hundred and fifty years old. I would be its twenty-ninth pastor. It would mean a Southern California boy moving his family to the northeastern United States, two regions separated by much more than miles.

So Lauretta and I went away for two days to pray for the essence of the Southern California I loved. For two days we walked the beaches and prayed and talked. But we heard nothing from God. The last evening we were there, we were having dessert at a Marie Callender's restaurant on the island. I was eating my favorite, apricot pie a la mode, as Lauretta and I discussed the situation. Then God spoke. It was as if, as I talked, I detached from my head and was hovering about two feet above me and slightly to my right. God was standing at my side.

He said, "You're resisting me, Ben."

I said, "I know."

He said, "It's because you don't want to go through the pain of saying good-bye to your friends."

I said, "That's true."

Then he said, "But that's not a good enough reason to say no to me."

I interrupted Lauretta and said, "God is calling us to go to New Jersey."

She said, "I know."

We both burst into tears. Some of mine fell into the pie.

What a ride it has been since then—desperately difficult, incredibly interesting, and, yes, hilarious—I mean, apricot pie a la mode? The Steven Curtis Chapman song says it all for Lauretta and me: "There's no better place to be than on the road to heaven, with Jesus by our side, our *paraclete*, whispering in our ears, leading us on."[12]

---

[12]"No Better Place," sung by Steven Curtis Chapman, *For the Sake of the Call*, Sparrow Song, 1990; words by Steven Curtis Chapman.

10

VECTORING PRAYER

EAST INDIAN EVANGELIST K. P. Yohannan says he will never forget one of his first prayer meetings in an American church. He had come to the United States eager to meet some of its spiritual giants and leaders. One man in particular held his interest, a preacher known even in India for his powerful sermons and uncompromising commitment to the truth. More than three thousand people attended services on the Sunday Yohannan visited his church. The choirs were outstanding and the preaching was everything he'd hoped it would be. But he was especially taken by an announcement the pastor made about the special emphasis at the midweek prayer meeting. He said there were some things lying heavy on his heart—would the people come and pray about them? Then he announced the name of a certain chapel on the church campus. Excited, Yohannan determined he would attend.

When he arrived at the chapel later that week, he brought with him some definite assumptions about prayer meetings. The most basic was that they are essential, of primary importance. Where he came from in India, and in many other parts of the world where Christians are persecuted and harassed for their faith, the prayer meeting is the centerpiece of the church's life. Everyone comes, the meetings often last long into the night, and it is not unusual for believers to arise daily before sunup to pray together for the work of the church.

Fearing a huge crowd, he came early to get a seat. But when he arrived he was surprised to discover a chapel with a capacity for only five hundred—that was empty! Surely he heard the pastor wrong and had come to the wrong place. He was worried, so he went outside to double-check the name of the chapel. Then a few people came into the room at 7:30, but there was no leader, no songs or worship, just chitchat about news, weather, and sports. Forty-five minutes later an elderly man, the leader, but not the pastor, walked into the chapel to offer a few devotional thoughts from the Bible and give a brief prayer. The meeting was over, and as the seven attendees filed out of the chapel, K. P. Yohannan sat in stunned silence, his mind filled with questions: *Was this it? Weren't they going to stay and wait upon God? Where was the worship? The tears? The cries for guidance and direction? Where was the list of the sick, and the poor, and those in need? What about that burden that the pastor said was heavy on his heart? Weren't we going to intercede for a miracle? And where was the pastor?*[1]

False sufficiency

That meeting became a paradigm for his experience of prayer meetings in the American church. In all his travels here, he saw the same pattern repeated over and over again in hundreds of midweek prayer meetings. Almost anything

---

[1]Source unknown.

happens but prayer. There are announcements, singing, homilies, and a few prayers offered, but usually only by the leader—and that's in the churches that actually have prayer meetings in their schedules. Many more make no pretense even to have a church prayer meeting. There seems to be time for everything else—to study, to fellowship, to preach, but not to pray. Church leaders who think nothing of spending two or three days to plan programs or of spending thousands of dollars to hire consultants to help them do it, blanch at the thought of spending even one night to wait on the Lord to show them what to do.

How can this be?

If it is true that "our struggle is not against flesh and blood, but against the rulers, against the authorities, against the powers of this dark world and against the spiritual forces of evil in the heavenly realms" (Eph. 6:12), then we must pray, mustn't we? Can there be any other way to reach a lost world? Do we really think our plans and programs can bring down dark strongholds of spiritual evil in the heavenly realms?

Yohannan attributes our prayerlessness to a false sense of self-sufficiency. The Laodicean church is *déjà vu* all over again in the so-called Christian West. That was the church that said of itself, "I am rich; I have acquired wealth and do not need a thing." But Jesus had a different opinion. *Au contraire*: "You do not realize that you are wretched, pitiful, poor, blind and naked." And worst of all, he saw himself as standing outside the church, not inside; knocking on the door, asking to be let in. "Here I am! I stand at the door and knock. If anyone hears my voice and opens the door, I will come in and eat with him, and he with me" (Rev. 3:14–22). To pray would be to open the door. But our sense of self-sufficiency paralyzes the hand that would turn the knob.

This, of course, is nothing less than blatant idolatry: "My people have exchanged their Glory for worthless idols"—buildings, machines, technology, programs, money. "They have forsaken me, the spring of living water, and have dug their own cisterns, broken cisterns that cannot hold water" (Jer. 2:11–13).

Earlier in this book, I identified some of the reasons for this apostasy. Secularization, the process by which things like prayer are losing their practical social significance, is at the root of most of our difficulties with prayer. For many of us, on an almost subconscious level, there is a lack of confidence that something like prayer can actually get anything done. Therefore, since our lives are full of things that need to be done, prayer naturally gets pushed out to the edges of the day. Prayer may have some therapeutic value; for instance, it can give one a sense of inner peace, but we think it can do little to raise money for the operating budget.

Believing there is not time to pray is a self-fulfilling prophecy; for the logic of secularization is to make us frenetically busy, overcommitted, and, finally, so full of blind activity that we become too busy and too tired to pray. As P. T. Forsyth warned, the inability to pray is the punishment for the refusal to pray. God said it would be that way: " 'In repentance and rest is your salvation, in quietness and trust is your strength, but you would have none of it. You said, "No, we will flee on horses." *Therefore you will flee!*' " (Isa. 30:15–16, italics mine). Flight is a good image of the kind of activity that dominates prayerless peoples and churches.

But the demise of corporate congregational prayer needs some special treatment. Along with secularization, American individualism has taken its toll. If churches fancy themselves self-sufficient, it's because their members share the same conceit about themselves. We like our lives to be self-contained. For many, the prayer meeting is unnecessary as long as individuals are praying in their own homes on their own time. What is missed is that most of what the Bible says about prayer is addressed to groups of people, meeting as groups to pray. The Bible's great book of prayer, the Psalms, was written largely for use in the congregation of Israel.

Even the individual prayer of a man like Ezra had the effect of moving all the people to pray together. For "while Ezra was praying and confessing, weeping and throwing himself down before the house of God, a large crowd of Israelites—men, women and children—gathered around him. They too wept bitterly" (Ezra 10:1). Unforgettable is the prayer life of the young church in Jerusalem, as "they all joined together constantly in prayer," and who, when threatened with persecution, "raised their voices together in prayer to God" for him to show his power against their enemies (Acts 1:14; 4:23–31). It was in a congregational prayer meeting that a missionary movement was launched in Antioch: "While they were worshiping the Lord and fasting, the Holy Spirit said, 'Set apart for me Barnabas and Saul for the work to which I have called them.' So after they had fasted and prayed, they placed their hands on them and sent them off" (Acts 13:1–3). When Paul urged the churches to pray for him, he was urging congregations to pray as congregations, not only as individuals.

Corporate shalom

Corporate prayer has a special place in God's heart because he desires that his people be one. Typically, Christians call the "Our Father" prayer the Lord's Prayer. But strictly speaking, that prayer should be called the disciples' prayer. The real Lord's Prayer is found in the seventeenth chapter of John where Jesus prays to the father, "I in them and you in me. May they be brought to complete unity to let the world know that you sent me and have loved them even as you have loved me" (John 17:23). Note that Jesus claims for Christian unity a power he gives only to the Holy Spirit, to nothing and no one else—the power to persuade the world that he is indeed the One sent from God, *"to let the world know that you sent me."* The greatest argument for the authority and identity of Jesus does not have to come from philosophers and theologians and apologists. It can come from the simplest believers who will live together in the unity of the Holy Spirit!

Why does unity have this kind of power? One reason is that when we live together in love and harmony, it can mean but one thing: that each of us has ceased being his own lord and has submitted himself or herself to the Lord. In such a state there can be no place for isolated individualism, the attitude Archbishop William Temple penned when he said, tongue-in-cheek, "I believe in one holy, infallible church, of which I regret to say that at the present time I am the only member."[2] R. H. Tawney was speaking in the same tone when he wrote, "The man who seeks God in isolation from his fellows is likely to find, not God, but the devil, who will bear an embarrassing resemblance to himself."[3] The lordship of Jesus Christ is meant to start in the church and to radiate out to the rest of the world. When Jesus is truly Lord over his people, his power is released.

There comes with this unity a quality in the church that only can be called precious. Jesus adds to its power to

---

[2]Source unknown.
[3]Source unknown.

convince the world of who he is, the power to convince it of who we are. "May they be brought to complete unity to let the world know that you sent me and *have loved them even as you have loved me*." In other words, he also claims for unity the power to persuade the world that we are indeed his people, precious to God and dearly loved by him. There is a blessedness, a shalom, among those who are one in Christ that is so extraordinary and miraculous that it is visible to nonbelievers.

"How good and pleasant it is," says Psalm 133, "when [kindred] live together in unity!" My friend Roderick Caesar likes to say of this psalm that most things are either good but not pleasant—like cleaning a toilet—or pleasant but not good—like eating too much apple pie. How few things are *both* good and pleasant!

What does this have to do with corporate prayer?

There can't be one without the other—no genuine corporate prayer without unity, no real unity without corporate prayer. If prayer is the deepest communion we can have with our Father God this side of heaven, how can we have this intimacy if we are at loggerheads with other brothers and sisters in his family? It can't be done. When we are less than one with each other, our oneness with Jesus is broken and incomplete. So then are our prayers. That's why Paul says to Timothy, "I want men everywhere to lift up holy hands in prayer," and then adds, "without anger or disputing" (1 Tim. 2:8).

Sören Kierkegaard said Jesus does two things when he sees a crowd: The first is to disperse it and isolate each individual one-on-one with himself. Having done that, the second thing he does is to reintroduce all these individuals to one another as brothers and sisters, making a crowd into a community. A true Christian community is always a community of prayer.

Our failure at corporate prayer is first a failure in Christian community to truly *agree* in the Lord. Taking his cue from the words of Jesus in Matthew 18:19, Jonathan Edwards urged the churches of eighteenth-century New England to see prayer as a kind of concert. "Again, I tell you, that if two of you agree about anything you ask for, it will be done for you by my Father in heaven." The word for "agree" is the Greek *sumphoneo*, from which we get our word "symphony." Edwards proposed that churches pray in concerted agreement for two things: the revival of religion in the church, and the spread of God's kingdom in the world. The Great Awakenings of the eighteenth and nineteenth centuries were birthed in this kind of prayer. With them came spiritual renewal and profoundly beneficial social and political changes.

That kind of praying required a level of Christian community most churches know nothing of.

Bob Bakke, of National Prayer Advance, tells of churches of Ipswich, Massachusetts, and their experience of this kind of prayer. After the first Great Awakening, three churches in this community covenanted to follow the pattern suggested by Edwards. In each congregation, cell groups would meet weekly to agree in prayer. Monthly, the separate congregations would then gather the cells and conduct all-church prayer meetings of agreement. Then quarterly, all three would come together for the same kind of praying. This pattern was followed faithfully, without interruption, for a century. Two remarkable things happened during this time. All three churches reported periodic harvest or "ingatherings" of souls, in which there would be a number of new believers brought into the congregations, about every eight to ten years. Also, during this time, all of New England was being swept by Unitarianism. But not these three churches. They remained firmly true to the faith while apostasy swirled around them, but not over them. Around the time of the Civil War, the prayer meetings ceased. Within five years these churches all capitulated to Unitarianism![4]

In times of intense spiritual conflict, simple, unified corporate prayer can be literally the difference between life and death.

Moravian Pentecost

The story of the Moravian Brethren is a similar one. When the Christians of various and disparate traditions—Roman Catholic, Calvinist, Lutheran, Anabaptist, and many others—gathered together on the Von Zinzendorf estate in Moravia, in the early 1700s, they saw themselves as pilgrims in spiritual unity. The Reformation had gone sour in many ways, with the church splintering into still more divisions, and all at war with one another. These people purposed to live together in such a way as to answer Jesus' prayer in John 17:23, and be brought to complete unity. They also had a mission motive, for they believed that such unity would persuade the world that Jesus was who he said he was. With many other Europeans of their era, they had a new and heightened sense of the vastness and diversity of the planet, and they wanted Christ to be confessed by every nation as Lord.

But within a few weeks, they were at each others' throats, fighting as badly as everyone else. Von Zinzendorf and the elders of the community were heartbroken. In desperation, they called for concerted prayer that God would send a new Pentecost to their community and heal their divisions and make them one, so the whole world would

---

[4]Bob Bakke, from a personal conversation.

165

know that Jesus is Lord. To this end, they instituted a twenty-four-hour prayer vigil—two women and two men praying each hour. Their prayers were answered as a powerful Pentecostal experience came on their community, and they were brought to repentance and harmony with one another in the Holy Spirit. Like the churches of Ipswich, the Moravians continued to pray twenty-four hours a day, with no break, for one hundred years! Wherever a Moravian community was established, twenty-four-hour concerted prayers was also established. During this time, two thousand missionaries went out from their communities to almost every corner of the earth.

It was in a Moravian prayer meeting on Aldersgate Street in London that a failed and discouraged missionary named John Wesley felt his heart "strangely warmed," and the Wesleyan revivals were birthed.

In a less dramatic, but no less profound way, Benedictine monks have carried on for centuries the same ministry of prayer in the unity of the Spirit. In chapter 2, I narrate the story of how my wife and I, while on a long and boring drive across the plains of North Dakota in 1975, discovered a Benedictine monastery. We poked around the grounds until we met one of the brothers who kindly took us on a tour. The monks carried on a vital ministry of prayer and worship as they farmed, conducted spiritual retreats, made crafts, and offered spiritual counsel to people from the region.

When I got home I found out a little bit more about the Benedictines. Founded by St. Benedict of Nursia in the sixth century, the order was formed as a creative response to the worldliness he saw that had crept into the church of his times. The first monastery was built on Monte Cassino in Italy. St. Benedict believed that the chief end, the chief work of man was to worship God, and that his community should therefore make worship and prayer central to its life. But he also believed that if prayer were the chief work, then work itself could become prayer, thus giving meaning to common labor. Rene Dubos, the French biologist, thinks that if environmentalism needs a patron saint, St. Benedict, much more than St. Francis, is the man.

I have believed ever since that the church should make the uncommon practice of the Benedictines common. There must be a way for all believers to integrate prayer and work in a community of love and unity. For what other reason would Jesus command it? These three, the pilgrims in Moravia, the Protestants in Ipswich, and the monks on Monte Cassino are but a few models of that earnest hope.

Good conversation

I was raised in a tradition that believed the man alone on his knees in the closet is the pinnacle of great prayer— one person one-on-one with the Almighty. Like Moses on Sinai. I still think that is extremely important. But the cutting edge of my personal prayer life lately has been in corporate prayer. I didn't understand this very well when I was growing up. I grew up in a church that had midweek prayer meetings, much like the one described by K. P. Yohannan. I hated them. Now I realize that good corporate prayer can demand more of us spiritually than individual prayer does. When I'm alone with God, I don't have to deal with other people. Frankly, I like God a lot more than I like some people. But the Lord is clear: if we love him, we must love others. Thus joining my heart with others before the throne of his grace is a way of loving God.

In many ways, the same rules that apply to good conversation apply to good corporate prayer. When our kids were young, it was a big deal just to get them to wait their turn to speak in dinner conversations. When that happened we were pleased, but we still had a long way to go, for then the conversations, though orderly, were a string of non sequiturs. Dan would go into excruciating detail to tell us his dream of the night before. Joel would politely wait his turn to tell us, immediately after Dan was done, that he had a yellow T-shirt in his closet. Andy would sit sucking his fingers, with a faraway look in his eyes, and when his turn came would grunt that he wanted a slingshot for his birthday. By the time Mary came along, we had advanced beyond that (somewhat!).

Some group prayer meetings are like that kind of conversation. We come together to the throne of God, or do we? Are we more like children waiting in line to speak to a department store Santa? We're occupying the same space, but we're not together. I've prayed countless times with adults and found myself just taking my turn, along with the rest of them, to say to God the things I wanted to say, without much thought for what others were praying.

Good corporate prayer is like good conversation. Through my wife's involvement in the Mom's In Touch prayer movement, I have learned a method that we call "agree, vector, and build." The method is to listen, really listen to a person's prayer, and to let it sink into my mind and heart before I move onto my particular concerns. For instance, someone may pray for a family member's health. As I mull over that prayer, I will add a kind of amen to it, *agreeing* with it, verbally or silently, thus entering more deeply into the concern. Sometimes when I do that, I may find myself moved to add my own prayer, a nuance, to the prayer I heard. Others may do the same, *vectoring* in their prayers and *building* on the original prayer.

When I have done this kind of praying in a group, it is remarkable the way we have experienced the leading of the

Holy Spirit—not only in how to pray for a matter but in what to do about it after we have. Along these lines, I have also heard my friend Bob Bakke urge prayer groups to make their prayers short and many. Long, sonorous prayers by the "adept" usually have the effect of stifling the participation of those who don't feel so adept at group prayer. So each should pray short prayers, many times in the course of a prayer session, thus leaving space for everyone to agree with, vector in, and build on the prayers of others. It can be a wonderful way to practice the *sumphoneo* the Lord commands.

Good corporate prayer in a large group also requires planning, at least as much as would go into any other well-planned service of worship. Many prayer meetings fail precisely at this point. For some reason the idea is out there that a prayer meeting should simply "flow" spontaneously in the Spirit, meaning that there should be no planning, since planning would somehow stifle the flow. That's not spontaneity, but what Thomas Howard calls the *myth* of spontaneity. The result is that the "adept" dominate the praying and the whole focus of the gathering sinks to the lowest common denominator. Our experience in other areas of life tells us that not much good comes from mere spontaneity. Ask the Mozarts and Einsteins of history if mere spontaneity had anything to do with their accomplishments, and they'll say hard work, yes; discipline, yes; but mere spontaneity, no. Perhaps their insights came in a flash that was experienced as spontaneity, but it was built on years of hard work and discipline. For that reason, I think it is a good idea for all-church prayer meetings to be significant worship events, taking place perhaps only monthly, rather than weekly, with small groups filling that slot.

Beyond meetings where the church gathers specifically

for prayer, prayer can also make a difference where the church gathers specifically for business.

I saw this work to great effect in my last two congregations. In both churches, elders' meetings tended to go long and late. So I proposed that we begin the meetings with the first hour devoted to prayer. At first the elders balked, reasoning that an hour of prayer would add an hour to the meeting. I argued that it would produce the opposite, that praying would help us get our work done faster, that instead of our meetings ending at what had become the "baseline" time of 11 P.M., they would end sooner.

They did, not always, but more than ever before. One reason may be because we were recognizing that the church is God's, not ours, and that since he's the head of the church, shouldn't we check in with him and sit in his presence before we presumed to conduct his business? It wasn't long before we also found ourselves stopping for prayer in the midst of a meeting, whenever we came to a point where we couldn't agree. Like so many in the Western church, we had been leading as practical deists, acting as though God had given us a package of resources—brains, Bible, finances, and facilities—and had walked away, leaving it to us to figure out what to do with it all. But the church is Christ's *body*, not his legacy; and we pray not for the sake of efficiency, because it gets the work done better, but for the sake of the truth, because he is its head.

Launch into the deep

After his experience in that disastrous, and all too common, midweek prayer meeting, K. P. Yohannan said he feared we were in danger of fathering an Ishmael. Ishmael, you will remember, was a child born of practical deists. When Abram and Sarai didn't see God's promise fulfilled in the time they expected, they took matters into their own hands, and Abram had intercourse with Hagar. They opted for the child of human calculation over the child of God's promise. Ishmael was the result, "a wild donkey of a man" (Gen. 16:12), at war with everyone.

I think prayerless churches have fathered many Ishmaels in their history, with the most visible result being their shameful divisions. As Ishmael mocked Isaac, the practical deists will mock those who prayerfully wait for the child of promise as ethereal and impractical, hopelessly out of touch with the real world. God was patient with all who were involved in the fiasco then: Abram and Sarai, Hagar and Ishmael. He waited until they learned to wait, and finally gave them what he had promised. I pray he will continue to do so with us.

I have written this book in the hope that somehow I can whet your appetite to read more, and above all, to pray more. Since the best teacher of prayer is the Holy Spirit, the best way to learn to pray is by praying. Whether, and how much we pray is, I think, finally a matter of appetite, of hunger for God and all that he is and desires. C. S. Lewis wrote in *The Weight of Glory*: "We are far too easily pleased." That, in the end, is the reason we do not pray more than we do. Nothing less than infinite joy is offered us in God's kingdom of light. He has promised that we will one day shine like the sun in that kingdom (Matt. 13:43).

We have become satisfied with mere church, mere religious exertion, mere numbers and buildings—the things we can do. There is nothing wrong with these things, but they are no more than foam left by the surf on the ocean of God's glory and goodness. There are things way out in the depths that only God can give us. They can be ours only if we launch out in our little prayer boats and learn to sail, even one day walk, on those waters.

Bon voyage, my friend.